STRANGE BUT TRUE

Ghost Sightings

STRANGE BUT TRUE

Ghost Sightings

COLIN WILSON

PARRAGON

This edition published and distributed by
Parragon
Unit 13–17, Avonbridge Trading Estate
Atlantic Road
Avonmouth
Bristol BS11 9QD

This edition produced by Magpie Books, an imprint
of Robinson Publishing Ltd., in 1997

British Library Cataloguing-in-Publication Data
A catalogue record for this book is available
from the British Library

ISBN 0–75252–132–2

Printed and bound in the E.C.

Contents

1   Spirits Without Bodies?

2   The Poltergeist

3   Spooks and Hobgoblins

4   Ghost Hunters

5   Ghost Detectives

6   Possession?

7   What is a Ghost?

Index

1

Spirits Without Bodies?

*Colonel Philip Meadows Taylor was a British officer who
served in India during the nineteenth century. He is now
remembered mainly for his powerful novel,* Confessions
of a Thug. *But in his autobiography,* The Story of my
Life, *he explains why he remained unmarried until fairly
late in life. It was, he said, "the result of a very curious and
strange incident that befell me during one of my marches to
Hyderabad."*

Apparitions

He had, he wrote, been deeply in love with a girl in
England, and had been hoping to propose to her
when they received an order that no soldier was to
be allowed to go on leave to Europe that year. "One
evening I was at the village of Dewas Kudea, after a
very long afternoon and evening march from Muktul,
and I lay down very weary; but the barking of village
dogs, and the baying of jackals, and the over-fatigue
and heat, prevented sleep, and I was wide awake and
restless. Suddenly, for my tent door was open, I saw
the face and figure so familiar to me, but looking older
and with a sad and troubled expression – the dress was

white and seemed covered with a profusion of lace, and glittered in the bright moonlight. The arms were stretched out and a low plaintive cry of, "Do not let me go; do not let me go!" reached me. I sprang forward but the figure receded, growing fainter and fainter till I could see it no longer, but the low sad tones still sounded. I had run barefoot across the open space where my tents were pitched, very much to the astonishment of the sentry on guard, but I returned to my tent without speaking to him.

"I wrote to my father, I wished to know whether there was any hope for me. He wrote back to me these words, 'Too late, my dear son – on the very day of the vision you describe to me, A. was married.'"

Until the very last words of the story, the reader probably wonders whether the father is about to say that Miss A. died at the moment the Colonel saw her. For this is, in fact, one of the commonest types of ghost – the person who is seen at the moment of death by relatives or close friends.

Compare it, for example, with the story told by the famous statesman, Lord Henry Brougham. He tells how, in December 1799, he was travelling in Sweden with some friends. "We set out for Gothenburg, determining to make for Norway. At about 2.00 a.m., arriving at a decent inn, we decided to stop for the night. Tired with the cold of yesterday, I was glad to take advantage of a hot bath before I turned in and here a most remarkable thing happened to me . . . . while lying in it and enjoying the comfort of the heat, after the late freezing I had undergone, I turned my head round, looking towards the chair on which I had deposited my clothes as I was about to get out of the bath. On the chair sat [my friend] G., looking calmly at me. How I got out of the bath, I know not, but on recovering my senses I found myself sprawling on the floor. The apparition, or whatever it was, that had taken the likeness of G. had disappeared.

"Soon after my return to Edinburgh, there arrived a letter from India announcing G.'s death, stating that he had died on the 19th December!"

Lord Brougham explains that at school G. was his most intimate friend, and that they frequently discussed the possibility of life after death. "We actually committed the folly of drawing up an agreement, written with our blood, to the effect that whichever of us died the first should appear to the other, and thus solve any doubts we had entertained of the 'life after death.'"

It is interesting to compare these two stories. The girl that Meadows Taylor loved was evidently not happy at getting married to another man, and probably experienced an intense feeling of misery while she was getting dressed for the wedding. (We should recall that the time in India is several hours ahead of London, and that when the Colonel was lying in bed, it was probably morning in England.) Somehow, her misery communicated itself to Meadows Taylor who actually saw her wearing her wedding dress.

In the same way, Lord Brougham's friend G., on his deathbed, probably remembered his promise to communicate with his old schoolfriend and as he was dying, made some kind of strange effort which actually made Lord Brougham aware of him.

Now compare that with a story told by the famous

Scottish lawyer Lord Erskine. Erskine tells how when he was a young man, he returned to Edinburgh after a long absence and "as I was coming out from a bookshop, I met our old family butler. He looked greatly changed, pale, wan and shadowy. 'Eh, old boy!,' I said, 'what brings you here?' He replied: 'To meet your honor and to solicit your interference with my lord to recover a sum due to me, which the steward at the last settlement did not pay.'

"Struck by his looks and manner, I bade him follow me to the booksellers shop into which I stepped back, but when I turned round to speak to him he had vanished. I remembered that his wife carried on some little trade in the Old Town, and I remembered the house. Having made it out, I found the old woman in widow's mourning. Her husband had been dead for some months, and had told her on his deathbed that my father's steward had wronged him out of some money but that when Master Tom returned he would see her righted. This I promised to do, and shortly after fulfilled my promise. The impression of this on me was indelible."

In other words, we now seem to have a case in which a man was so anxious to communicate with someone that he waited for several months until Lord Thomas Erskine returned before appearing to him.

All these stories are taken from a book called *Noted Witnesses for Psychic Occurrences*, by the American psychologist Walter Franklin Prince who died in 1934. Some of Prince's best known cases have a "psychic" element, particularly the case of a girl called Doris Fischer, who became Prince's adopted daughter.

Multiple Personality

Doris is a fascinating example of a strange psychological disorder which is today called "multiple personality syndrome" (MPD). Several people lived in her body at the same time.

Prince learned that the first sign of multiple personality appeared in 1892, when Doris was three-years-old. Her drunken father hurled her to the floor in a rage and the girl who sat up was no longer Doris, but another personality who later claimed that she was a spirit. Let us refer to her as Ariel.

As Doris started to go upstairs to bed, yet another personality suddenly took over – Margaret. It was Margaret who went upstairs and went to sleep, and the next morning came down the stairs. As she reached the foot of the stairs, there was a slight snap of the neck (as if an electric current had been turned on), and Doris suddenly found herself back in her own body. She had no memory of what had taken place since her father snatched her out of her mother's arms on her way to bed.

From then on, Mrs Fischer witnessed a peculiar change in her daughter. Sometimes Doris was the normal, quiet, studious little girl she had always known. At other times, she became a mischievous sprite – noisy, tomboyish, witty and amusing, an excellent mimic, and generally lovable. Mrs Fischer had no way of knowing that this was not Doris but another girl called Margaret.

Doris had no knowledge of the existence of Margaret. All she knew was that she would periodically "blank out", and often, when she came back to consciousness, she found herself in trouble for some mischievous prank. If she was reaching out for cake, Margaret might suddenly take over and gobble it down. Doris would return to consciousness as she was licking her lips. Yet, on the whole, Margaret was not ill-disposed to her. Later she told Doris all about herself, using Doris' mouth. The two of them would hold conversations, and Doris had no idea of what Margaret would say until it actually came out of her mouth. If Margaret wanted to speak to her when there were other people present, she simply put the words into Doris' mind, so that no one suspected that Doris was two people. One day, when Doris was five, she was playing with a rubber ball which Margaret felt belonged to her. Margaret made her pick the ball up, to draw attention to it, and then made her scratch herself on the cheek until she bled – it was Margaret's way of telling Doris to leave her toys alone.

In spite of these complications, Doris' childhood was not too unhappy. Ariel appeared at night when Margaret was asleep. (Doris continued to blank out as she reached the top of the stairs, and to reappear the next morning.) It was rather as if Doris had a mischievous twin sister who was always getting her into trouble – and sometimes helping her out of it. Margaret often did her school work for her. But her recklessness was sometimes dangerous – Mrs Fischer could never understand why Doris would go swimming in the docks after solemnly promising not to.

The first real conflict occurred when Doris was in her mid-teens. She had graduated almost at the top of her class, and decided to go on to high school. Margaret flatly refused. The conflict would have made life impossible, so Doris left school and – reluctantly – went to work as a seamstress. When she was seventeen, she was at work one day when she had several hallucinations showing that her mother was seriously ill. She rushed home to find her mother dying, although she had been well that morning. It was sudden acute pneumonia. By 2.00 a.m. the following morning, her mother was dead. Her father staggered home drunk (while she sat by the bedside of her dying mother) and slumped into bed fully dressed, without even noticing that his wife was dead. As Doris drew the sheet over her mother's face, she experienced a sudden pain in her head – and another personality was looking out through her eyes. This new person had no memory at all. She suddenly came to birth sitting by a bed that contained a dead woman in her nightgown, and a fully dressed man. She was not afraid or worried because she had no idea of what death was. In the next room, Doris' sister Trixie – also ill – woke up and called "Doris!," but the new personality in Doris' body had no idea who Doris was.

Although Doris had attended to her dying mother, Margaret was also there, "underneath", watching it all and sympathizing with Doris' splitting headache. When Doris had finished laying out the corpse, Margaret made a brief appearance, immediately felt the headache, and beat a quick retreat. Then, to Margaret's surprise, the "other" person suddenly appeared in Doris' body. "What a dumb thing that new one was," she later told Prince. "She didn't seem to know *anysing*." (Margaret had a kind of childish lisp.)

Margaret found herself sharing Doris' body with another inmate who was unable to read, write or talk – who was basically a kind of new-born baby. She decided to make the best of it and teach the newcomer to speak. This was slightly easier than it would have been in the case of two separate people, for even when the newcomer was in control of the body, Margaret would make her lips move to repeat words. She taught her the name of objects by pointing at them, and the newcomer repeated the names after her.

Prince called the newcomer "Sick Doris." Even when she had learned to speak, she was obviously an inferior personality. Her face was wooden and dull, she was afraid to meet people's eyes, her voice was monotonous and she was shy, nervous and incapable of affection – although she could sustain a dog-like friendship. She was religious in a stupid kind of way, literal-minded and inclined to hysteria and various aches and pains. Since Prince emphasizes that she was a completely separate personality, we will here refer to her as Mary Anne.

When Doris was eighteen, she slipped and fell on the back of her head. This brought into existence yet another personality, on a still-lower scale than any so far, a partial individual who appeared only when Doris was asleep. Margaret, who observed the appearance of this newcomer one night, referred to her as "Sleeping Real Doris," but this is inaccurate since she was not "Real Doris" in any sense – we will simplify by calling her Jane. Jane was basically little more than a tape recorder – she would accurately "replay" whole conversations dating back to Doris' childhood with all the facial expressions of a seven-year-old girl. Prince quotes conversation between Doris and her mother – recited by Jane – in which Doris spoke only her own part and left silences as her mother replied.

And so, by the age of eighteen, Doris was a walking compendium of personalities – herself, Margaret, Ariel, Mary Anne and Jane. In the following year, she met Mrs Prince and began to go to the Princes' for meals. Finally, she moved in with them and became a kind of adopted daughter. In these new and delightful living conditions, with the constant attention of Dr Prince, her mental health began to improve steadily, so that it is possible that even without treatment, she would have recovered. By 1914, Doris was back in sole control, although Margaret continued to pay occasional visits simply out of friendliness. When she first moved into the Princes' house, Doris had almost disappeared. The chief personality was Margaret – a pleasant girl whose development had ceased, unfortunately, at the age of ten – who alternated with a lumpish Mary Anne.

The first thing Prince observed was that he was dealing with two completely different girls. This is apparent even from their photographs, which appeared in Prince's paper about the case in *The Journal of Abnormal Psychology*, in 1916. There is only a family resemblance. On her very occasional appearances, Doris was different from both. Even their physical characteristics were different. Doris had little or no sense of taste or smell. Prince said she suffered from anaesthesia in the bladder, by which he means, presumably, that she was unaware of the normal sensations when her bladder was full and was inclined to wet herself. Mary Anne seems to have had no nerves in her skin below the waist and not many above it. Margaret, on the other hand, not only had unusually sharp hearing, but could also see in the dark.

The different personalities would take over with a slight "click" in the neck. It really looked as though there were several persons making use of Doris' body, as several members of a family might make use of one car. The various personalities even talked about being "in" and "out," and Margaret would often remark that she was allowing Doris to rest while she took over. Margaret also told Prince that she could "duck under" – that is, abandon Doris' body while Doris was not yet in control. She did this occasionally by way of demonstration – then Doris' body would lie still, hardly breathing, apparently in a cataleptic trance.

Prince observed that the various personalities seemed to be in a definite hierarchy of "higher" and "lower." At the bottom of the ladder (my phrase, not his), was the "tape-recorder", Jane. Next came Mary Anne, then Margaret, then Doris, then Ariel. Ariel, who appeared when Doris was asleep, seemed to know more than any of them and claimed that she was a spirit who had come in answer to fervent prayers of Doris' mother to protect her daughter.

Doris knew nothing about any of the other personalities, at least, by direct insight or memory. Margaret could "read the minds" of Doris and Mary Anne, but was unaware of the existence of Ariel. This led to some minor tension between Prince and Margaret. If Margaret had been in Doris' body too long, Ariel got annoyed and gave her a blow on the forehead – or at least produced the hallucination of giving her a blow. The startled Margaret would imagine that Prince had hit her, and shrink away from him – his denials were obviously regarded as lies. These "jolts" (as Ariel called them), failed to achieve the desired effect – understandably, since Margaret had no idea why she was being hit – and Ariel finally promised to stop it. Thereafter, the "jolts" ceased.

Margaret finally realized that there must be some personality of whom she was unaware. One day, when Doris was "in," Margaret suddenly took over and started to talk to Prince. Ariel grabbed Margaret by the scruff of the neck and dragged her back "into the depths," allowing Doris to reappear. Later, the round-eyed Margaret told Doctor Prince, "Papa, there's another Sick Doris [Mary Anne], there's another Sick Doris! There must be, 'cause I was yanked in just the way I used to yank Sick Doris." But Ariel kept her interference to a minimum – apparently she found it an exhausting effort.

The relationship between the various personalities was, on the whole, what one might expect. Margaret could read Doris' and Mary Anne's mind. Ariel could read both these and also Margaret's. Sometimes Doris would be watched by three alter-egos, although only Ariel was aware of the full situation. Each personality – except Jane – had a mind of its own. Occasionally, something like a quarrel would develop. Mary Anne would think wistfully that if Doris stayed away for good, she and Margaret could share the body and Margaret might come to like her as much as she liked Doris. Margaret would read this thought and get angry with Mary Anne. Ariel, in turn, would feel irritated with Margaret – Ariel apparently felt protective towards Mary Anne. Doris, vaguely disturbed by these tensions, would "vanish" and leave either Margaret or Mary Anne to take over.

To complicate matters, the relationships altered according to Doris' mental health – at times Ariel could read Doris' thoughts only by reading Mary Anne's mind. There were also occasions when two personalities were in control at once. Prince could converse with Margaret *and* Doris, who took turns speaking. Or sometimes Margaret and Mary Anne shared the "driving-seat." And on rare occasions, Margaret and Ariel shared. Since Margaret was unaware of the existence of Ariel, Prince had to devise a method of talking with Ariel "behind Margaret's back," getting Ariel to signal the answers to questions by movements of her feet, while Margaret was oblivious of what was going on (she had no nerves below the waist.)

When Doris came to live with the Princes' in 1910, at the age of 21, the cure began. Doris began to spend more and more time in control, and Mary Anne began to fade away. To encourage Mary Anne's departure, Prince prevented her from doing needlework, which had previously been her chief occupation. Without this aid to concentration, her mind began to wander (in effect she became an idiot.) She realized that she was going to die and went for a long last walk with

Prince. Then she wrote a letter to Margaret (the various personalities often communicated by leaving notes for one another), full of advice and telling Margaret what to do with her few possessions. After that Mary Anne ceased to recognize the Princes. She began "growing backwards", reverting to infancy until she could only prattle and gurgle. She "died" on June 28, 1911.

Jane, the tape-recorder, stayed around longer. Prince was curious about her – he wondered whether she could become a real person and tried to "bring her out". Jane proved to be so responsive that Prince decided to stop, since ultimately he wanted to get rid of her. Jane simply faded away, making her last appearance in April 1912.

As Doris's health and confidence increased, Margaret began to get younger and younger. She began using the German pronunciations of Doris's early childhood. Her visual field gradually narrowed – sometimes that had also happened to Mary Anne – so she could only see things little more than a foot away from her face. Light stung her eyes, and if no shade was interposed, she began to weep. Finally Margaret went blind. Two years after Jane had "died", Margaret appeared one evening, laughed and made a few remarks, then fell asleep. That was her last appearance.

There was no question of trying to "freeze out" Ariel. She had no intention of hanging on. Prince refers to her as "the maturest, wisest and most prescient of the quintet." In the evenings, after Doris had gone to sleep, Ariel would occasionally chat with Prince. She would also occasionally interfere while Doris was awake, to warn her of some emergency. Prince makes the extraordinary statement, "If I had not the experience of the first hand study of [Ariel] for years I would certainly be of the opinion that she represents a slight or deeply-seated remaining dissociation of personality; as it is, I have my doubts." That is to say, Prince was half-inclined to believe her claims that she was some sort of independent guardian spirit, not a "splinter" of Doris' personality.

In 1916, Doctor James Hyslop (one of the founder members of the American Society For Psychical Research), suggested that Prince should take Doris to New York to see a well-known spirit medium called Mrs Chenoweth. But Prince had to refuse – he had moved to California from Pittsburgh and could not spare the time. A few evenings later, Ariel suddenly spoke out of Doris' mouth and said, "Why not let *me*? I'll look after her." And because Prince trusted Ariel so much, he agreed. The result is that Doris went to New York in the autumn of 1914 and had a number of "sittings" with Mrs Chenoweth.

Mrs Chenoweth was a medium who went into a trance with a pencil in her hand, and the pencil answered questions in automatic writing. On that first day, Mrs Chenoweth was already in a trance when Doris came in and sat down beside her. But as soon as Doris sat down, the pencil began to move and wrote the name of Doris's father. Mrs Chenoweth had no idea of who was coming to see her that morning. And after that, a person who claimed to be Doris's mother began to write. She began by saying that she had not wanted to die because she had several plans which she wanted to carry out – which was certainly true of

Doris's mother, who, in spite of being married to a dipsomaniac, was a lively, cheerful sort of person who had many hopes for the future. Doris's mother – or someone claiming to be Doris's mother – then wrote out long messages in which she showed close knowledge of Doris's background and childhood. A "spirit" who appeared to be Margaret also put in an appearance. When asked about her after-life she replied drily, "I never had a before-life; how can I have an after-life?" And a spirit that identified itself as Dr Richard Hodgson, another famous American psychical researcher – now dead – appeared and made some interesting comparisons between the Doris case and another equally famous case of multiple personality, Morton Prince's Christine Beauchamp case. Hodgson had actually worked with Morton Prince on this case.

Perhaps the most interesting assertion made at these sittings was the claim of Doris's mother that Doris's illness was a case of "benevolent possession" – that is, that "Ariel" was actually some kind of spirit who had moved into her body to protect her. Unfortunately, Ariel failed to put in an appearance at these seances – probably bored with the whole thing – and so the last we hear of Doris is her return from New York to California, none the wiser about the nature of her strange illness.

What are we to make of all this? For the average reader, the case will appear so weird that it is difficult to relate it to the normal lives of normal human beings. Yet, although the case of Doris Fischer is remarkable, there are nevertheless hundreds of similar cases in medical records – many of which have been printed.

All of us think of ourselves as a single person living in the body in which we were born and finally "vanishing" when that body dies. The majority of doctors and psychologists would argue that a human being *is* his or her body, the various nervous circuits and brain cells that interact to create the personality. The Doris case seems to be a flat contradiction of this idea. It seems to tell us that several people can live in the same body, just as several people can live in the same house. But just as several people cannot use a telephone at the same time, so several people cannot use the brain and the voice that belong to the body they are all inhabiting. If the body is merely a kind of house, which can be used at different times by different people, this would also explain Lord Thomas Erskine's vision of his butler. The butler was anxious about the money that was owed to him, and after the death of his body he simply waited around until "Master Tom" came to Edinburgh, and then somehow managed to talk to him.

The case of Colonel Meadows Taylor has even stranger implications. It looks as if the girl Taylor was in love with – and who was obviously in love with him – somehow managed to "project" herself to India, to tell him that she didn't want to get married to someone else.

The case of Lord Brougham makes the same point. His friend G. had promised to try and communicate with him at the time of his death, and he appears to have succeeded. This can mean one of two things. Either that human beings possess powers of communication that they do not even suspect, or that our personalities continue to live on after our death and can somehow get in touch with people who are still alive. And of course there is no reason why both these things should not be true.

'I Am Two Women'

The Doris Fischer case is certainly unusual, but similar cases happen all the time. The *Sunday People* newspaper for November 4, 1979 had a headline, "I AM TWO WOMEN." The story, by William Munnings, runs:

"Medical scientists have told housewife Patricia McDonnell that she is not one person but *two*.

"Experts have discovered *two* blood groups in her body. And she has revealed that she has *two* different personalities.

"Mrs McDonnell, a 30-year-old mother, lives a perfectly normal life in Hollfast Road, Sutton Coalfield, in the West Midlands. But her case is extraordinary. 'We have told her that she is unique,' said Mr Bill Mortimer, consultant gynaecologist at the Good Hope Hospital, Sutton Coalfield.

"Doctors say that her mother should have had twins. Instead, baby Patricia absorbed the embryo of her twin into her own body. 'The foetus is still there, producing its own blood.'

"It was seven years ago, when Pat had her first child, Russell, that doctors discovered her double existence. 'A routine test showed two blood groups, groups O and A.'

" 'After that,' said Pat, 'there were countless tests on

my blood, saliva, hair and skin. Samples were sent all over the world. My mother and brother and sisters had tests as well. I thought I had some serious illness. I was terrified.'

"Then the doctors told her what they thought had happened at her birth. And they began to search for the twin embryo inside her. 'Every part of my body was X-rayed,' said Pat. 'But the doctors haven't found it because it keeps moving around. They asked me if I could feel it moving. After that I kept imagining I could. They cut off pieces of my hair to see if the texture varied. They checked whether I saw things differently through each eye. They thought one side of my body was different from the other. Then they asked if I had two personalities, which I have.

"'Sometimes I'm a cheerful extrovert, dashing about. Next day I will be an introvert, withdrawn, sitting in the house, not even washing dishes.

"'I can't switch deliberately from one personality to the other. It just happens.

"'I get days when I don't feel I am me.

"'When I am my "twin" I am allergic to my gold jewellery.

"'I get a rash on my neck and around my ears. My fingers swell up.

"'But when I change back to "me" the rash goes.' A scientific paper has been written about her called 'The Birmingham Chimaera,' after a fabled hybrid of Ancient Greece.

"'It is the first case of its kind for 25 years,' said gynaecologist Bill Mortimer, one of the authors of the paper. 'One of our theories is that the foetus of her twin is in her body, but we can't give a proper explanation. The genetics of this case are very complicated.'

"Another medical expert said, 'When this sort of thing happens, the person's health is not affected. And the children are perfectly normal.' At one stage, doctors were worried about what could happen when Pat has her change of life. Now they say her two blood groups will go on living happily together.

"'But I hope I never need large blood transfusions after an accident,' said Pat. 'I've had to give pints of blood which have been stored for my own use.'

"Six weeks ago, Pat had her second baby, Jolie. There were no problems.

"Before her confinement, Pat used to wonder if the 'twin' foetus was in her womb and if she would give birth to her twin.

"'But Jolie is obviously my baby,' said Pat, and she's really gorgeous.'

"Mrs Maisie Summers, Pat's mother, said she was startled when doctors told her of their belief that Pat had a twin foetus in her body.

"'As far as I'm concerned,' she said, 'my daughter Pat had a normal birth.'

"Doctors are baffled by the fact that Mrs Summers had apparently had an uncomplicated pregnancy and delivery with no sign of problem.

"So the origin of Pat's 'double life' remains a mystery."

Captain Frederick Marryat, the author of *Mr Midshipman Easy*, once had an interesting encounter with a ghost. It was at Raynham Fall in Norfolk, home of the Townshend family.

Sir Charles Townshend had just inherited the title and had invited various friends and neighbors to a party. But he noticed that the guests made an excuse to leave early. One of them finally admitted that they were nervous about the ghost of the "Brown Lady" who was believed to wander along the corridors. She was supposed to be Lady Dorothy Townshend, the sister of the Prime Minister, Sir Robert Walpole. She died in 1726 and is believed to have been deeply unhappy.

Sir Charles told Captain Marryat – who was a Justice of the Peace – about the haunting and Marryat decided that it was probably a trick devised by smugglers or poachers to try and drive the tenants away from Raynham Hall. Accordingly, he offered to spend three nights in the hall to try and lay the ghost.

Nothing happened for two nights. But on the third night, the baronet's two young nephews knocked on his door. They wanted to show him a gun they had just received from London. Marryat went to their room and looked at it, and then the two boys accompanied him back to his own room "just in case they met the Brown Lady."

At the end of a long corridor, they saw a light approaching. Marryat was dressed in shirt and trousers and regarded himself as "inappropriately dressed" to appear before a lady. So he ducked into a space between two doors, while the boys concealed themselves opposite. As the lady approached, Marryat realized with a shock that he had seen her portrait in one of the bedrooms – the portrait of Lady Dorothy Townshend.

In her account of the incident, Marryat's daughter Florence claims that the Brown Lady then stopped and disclosed a horrible malevolent face, at which Marryat fired his pistol at her. The truth is probably that he simply lost his nerve and fired. (The "malevolent face" is typical of the kind of embellishment that gets added to ghost stories.)

The Lady immediately disappeared. And the bullet was found later embedded in the door on the other side of the corridor.

There is a postscript to this story. On September 19, 1936, a photographer for *Country Life* was taking a picture of the main staircase at Raynham Hall while his assistant held a light. When the picture developed, it revealed the dim shape of a woman descending the stairs – a famous "spirit photograph" which is still frequently printed today.

Alter Egos?

In his book *Alter Egos* (1996), psychiatrist David Cohen tells some astonishing stories of patients he has dealt with. One of them, Jonah, a black youth from Kentucky, sounds very much like Doris Fischer. When he was six-years-old, Jonah's mother stabbed her husband in the course of a fight. One day, their six-year-old suddenly started to lecture them as if he was an adult. But according to Jonah, it was not his six-year-old self that lectured them. At the moment when his mother stabbed her husband, another personality suddenly took over Jonah's body – a personality that called itself Sammy. Sammy, like Ariel, seems to have been much more of an adult than Jonah, and it was he who told them that they should not behave so irresponsibly again.

Unfortunately, Jonah's mother had always wanted a girl, and she insisted on dressing him in girls' clothes. The result was that he was bullied at school, and the result of this mental stress was that, suddenly, yet another personality appeared – he called himself King Young. He was much more sophisticated than Jonah, and was something of a ladies' man.

One day, Jonah was chased by a gang of white boys who knocked him to the ground and started to beat him. Jonah was terrified. Suddenly, he blanked out and yet another personality entered his body. Quite suddenly, Jonah seemed to be transformed. He leapt to his feet and hurled himself at his tormentors, nearly killing two of them. The personality who had taken over his body claimed to be an African warrior king called Usoffa.

After a period in the army, during which Jonah went berserk on two occasions, he went home to Kentucky and suddenly woke up to find himself in jail. He had apparently beaten up a man and a woman in a bar – but had no memory of it. He was able to avoid standing trial. But two years later, when the police found him trying to drown a man in the river, he was given a short jail sentence. After that, Jonah went to hospital and tried to get medical treatment.

He had started attacking his wife with a kitchen knife, claiming that his real name was Usoffa. His wife had left him. Two days later, he tried to stab a complete stranger.

It can be seen that, in Jonah's case, the Multiple Personality Syndrome has produced some unpleasant and bewildering complications. At the time Cohen wrote about the case in his book, Jonah was still under treatment.

Cohen himself is inclined to think that Multiple Personality is rather like children playing games, enjoying pretending to be someone else. But we can see that that simple view does not seem to fit the case of Doris Fischer. In another of the cases he recounts, a girl he calls Lizzie makes it seem that his theory is rather too simplistic.

Lizzie was recommended to Cohen by another psychiatrist. She had made several attempts at suicide by slicing her wrists and had periods of depression, dizziness and blank spells. The police had picked her up a number of times, and she had no idea of how she had got to the place where they found her.

Cohen learned that Lizzie came from a religious family and that her father had been an important figure in the local Baptist Church. She had been good at Bible studies and won a number of scripture prizes. Her father and mother had a normal and happy marriage. The psychiatrist who had introduced Cohen to Lizzie was a man called Trevor. He described how Lizzie had gone missing and had been put on the missing person's register. But a police constable who had talked to Lizzie when she was being held overnight, told Trevor that Lizzie insisted he had got her name wrong. She wasn't called Lizzie. Her name was Esther.

When she finally reappeared, Trevor asked her where she had been for the last six months. She looked surprised. She thought she had last seen him about a month ago. Trevor asked her who Esther was – and he also mentioned another name that the policeman thought he had overheard – Faversham. Lizzie looked puzzled. The name seemed familiar, but she could not place it.

The next morning, at 7.00 a.m., Trevor got an early phone call from Lizzie. She had had a terrible nightmare about Esther, and in her nightmare, Esther was a witch who had been dead for 300 years. She lived in Faversham in Kent, and was not called Esther Faversham but Esther *of* Faversham. She had been burned at the stake there.

Trevor tried placing her under a very mild hypnosis and asked her whether she had ever been to Faversham. "I once went to Margate," said Lizzie. Margate is about 30 miles from Faversham. Apparently her grandmother might have taken her there – "We used to go on a lot of picnics."

Lizzie went on to explain that her grandmother was a very different kind of woman from her extremely religious parents. She was her father's mother and used to poke fun at him. She said he didn't know how to enjoy himself. Lizzie's grandmother had left her husband (who used to get drunk and beat her), and had taken up with a man called Victor, who was five years her junior. She and Victor used to work in the hop fields in Kent, and after winning some money on the horses, they bought a small boarding-house in Margate. Apparently, Lizzie's parents had allowed her to go down and stay with her grandmother quite frequently.

This struck Trevor as strange – that her strait-laced parents should allow her to go and stay with her disreputable grandmother. He asked her if she had annoyed them. She replied, "Mum and Dad only liked me when I was being a Bible girl." Her father would hit her for not obeying Jesus, and her mother. Her mother would arrange for her to go down to Kent to stay with her grandmother.

In another session of deep relaxation, Lizzie's voice suddenly changed – it seemed to become much deeper. She said, "If you want to find out about Esther why not ask her? Oh yes, Esther of Faversham. That's me." Esther went on to explain that she had been a witch in the seventeenth century and that she'd been burned. Her soul had survived and she had spent a long time waiting to return. Then she had decided to move into Lizzie's body. Esther was very concerned not to be burned again so she had chosen a religious girl. Esther now regretted it – she hated Lizzie's parents. "They were awful. Good people who did nothing but eat, piss and pray." It had been Esther who had often made Lizzie misbehave so that she was sent off to stay with her grandparents.

Trevor then asked her what had happened when she had been staying with her grandmother and Victor. One evening, when the grandmother was out shopping, Victor told Lizzie that he would help to dry her after a bath. "It had been 300 years since a man had touched me," Esther said. Victor had proceeded to seduce the little girl. It had started with him helping her wash and dry herself. Then he started reading stories to her as she lay in bed. Then he began getting her to masturbate him. And when she reached puberty, he came into her bedroom one night, put a hand over her mouth, and had sex with her. Esther didn't mind, she claimed, but Lizzie's reaction was very different.

This, it seemed, explains some of Lizzie's mental problems – psychiatrists have discovered that an enormous number of cases of Multiple Personality begin with childhood sexual abuse.

When Lizzie was 15, she discovered she was pregnant. Her parents believed that their daughter had simply been having sex with some local boy. But Lizzie denied she was pregnant. She had no memory whatever of the sex with Victor. Nevertheless, her parents sent her back down to Kent. Her grandmother, who suspected that Victor might be responsible for her state, sent her into a private hospital for an abortion. When she left hospital, she took a train back to her parents. But for some reason, she never arrived. Esther had intervened and taken control of her.

It was Esther who told Trevor what had happened next. She had stopped in London and joined a commune, including people who had been interested in astrology. Esther had been able to teach them something about it. And then, just as Esther was having the first good time she had experienced for 300 years, Lizzie started to come back. All that Lizzie could remember was getting back to her parents' house wearing flowered skirts and jewellery like a hippie.

Lizzie is confused about what happened next. She found herself in a psychiatric hospital and thinks that her parents put her there. At the first opportunity, Esther took over her body and walked out. From then on, Lizzie was in and out of psychiatric hospitals and had attempted suicide several times.

By this time, a third voice had begun to speak through Lizzie's mouth – apparently someone else who inhabited the body and who disliked Esther as much as Lizzie did. This third voice belonged to a person who was angry with Trevor – she felt that Trevor had not tried hard enough to get Lizzie better.

Cohen concludes by saying; "There is no happy ending to this case. Lizzie's GP is keeping her fairly heavily drugged, which has the effect of keeping Esther asleep. But Lizzie, although relieved not to have to struggle with Esther, is unhappy about the side effects of the drug."

And so Cohen finishes the story of Lizzie and Esther. Is it all a matter of illusion? Was Esther really a witch who was burned in Faversham 300 years ago, and who somehow managed to take over Lizzie's body? Cohen is obviously unwilling to believe this. But some of the evidence presented in this chapter makes it sound at least plausible.

2

The Poltergeist

The poltergeist or "noisy ghost" is one of the most baffling phenomena in the realm of the paranormal. There are thousands of people who do not believe in ghosts, but who will reluctantly admit that the evidence for the poltergeist is too strong to ignore. The favorite theory of such skeptics is that the poltergeist is some unexplained freak of the human mind.

If the poltergeist is a "ghost" or spirit, as its name implies, then its chief characteristic is as a spirit of mischief. Poltergeists cause objects to fly through the air, doors to open and close and pools of water to appear from nowhere. And they are by no means a rarity – at this very moment some case of poltergeist activity is probably going on within a dozen miles of the reader of this book. (I know of a case that is going on within a dozen miles of me as I write this.)

One of the earliest known cases was recorded in a chronicle called the *Annales Fuldenses*, dating back to AD 858. It took place in a farmhouse at Bingen, on the Rhine. The chronicle describes an "evil spirit" that "threw stones, and made the walls shake as if men were striking them with hammers." Stone-throwing is one of the most typical of poltergeist activities. The poltergeist also caused fires – another of their favorite activities (although, for some reason, they seldom do serious damage) – in this case burning the farmer's crops soon after they were gathered in. It also developed a voice (a much rarer feature in poltergeist cases), and denounced the man for various sins, including fornication and adultery. Priests sent by the Bishop of Mainz apparently failed to exorcise it – in fact, it is virtually impossible to get rid of a poltergeist by exorcism ceremonies.

It was only after the formation of the Society for Psychical Research in 1882, that the poltergeist was carefully studied. Then it was observed that in the majority of cases there were adolescent children present in the houses where such occurrences took place. It seemed a reasonable assumption that the children were somehow the "cause" of the outbreak. And in the age of Freud, the most widely-held theory was that the poltergeist is some kind of "unconscious" manifestation of adolescent sexual energies, but no one has so far offered a theory as to exactly how this can occur.

The Phantom Drummer of Tedworth

In England, one of the most spectacular cases is also one of the earliest to be thoroughly recorded – the so-called "Phantom Drummer of Tedworth." It took place in the home of a magistrate called John Mompesson in March 1661. The whole household was kept awake all night by loud drumming noises. The magistrate had been responsible for the arrest of a vagrant named William Drury, who attracted attention in the street by beating a drum. Mompesson had the drum confiscated, in spite of Drury's appeals. Drury escaped from custody – he was being held for possessing forged papers – without his drum. It was after this that the disturbances in Mompesson's household began and continued for two years. The "spirit" also slammed doors, made panting noises like a dog and scratching noises like huge rats, as well as purring noises like a cat. It also developed a voice and shouted, "A witch, a witch!" It emptied ashes and chamberpots into the children's beds, and caused various objects to fly through the air. In 1663, Drury, who was in prison for stealing a pig, admitted to a visitor that he was somehow responsible for the disturbances and said they would continue until Mompesson made him satisfaction for taking away his drum. But the phenomena finally seem to have faded away.

Old Jeffrey

A famous poltergeist haunting took place in the home of the Revd Samuel Wesley – grandfather of the founder of Methodism – at his rectory at Epworth in Lincolnshire. "Old Jeffrey", as the family came to call it, kept them awake on the night of December 1, 1716, with appalling groans and – a few nights later – with loud knocking noises. It also produced sounds of footsteps walking along the corridors and in empty rooms. The "focus" of the disturbances seemed to be

19-year-old Hetty Wesley, who was usually asleep when the disturbances began and who trembled in her sleep. As usual, the disturbances gradually faded away.

The "Cock Lane" Ghost

The famous case of the "Cock Lane" ghost ended with an innocent man going to prison for two years. The focus of these disturbances was ten-year-old Elizabeth Parsons, daughter of a clerk called Richard Parsons. The Parsons family had two lodgers – a retired innkeeper named William Kent and his common law wife, Fanny Lynes, whose sister Elizabeth had been Kent's previous wife. (This was why they could not marry, the law preventing a man from marrying his deceased wife's sister.) One night, when Kent was away, Fanny Lynes asked the ten-year-old girl to sleep with her to keep her company – they were kept awake by scratching and rapping noises from behind the wainscot. Soon after this, Fanny Lynes died of smallpox and Kent moved elsewhere. The strange rappings continued and a clergyman named Moore tried to communicate with the "spirit", using a code of one rap for yes, two for no. By this means, the "spirit" identified itself as Fanny Lynes and accused her "exhusband" of poisoning her with arsenic.

Parsons was unfortunately unaware that poltergeists tell lies more often than not. And he was not displeased to hear that Kent was a murderer, for he was nursing a grudge against him. Kent had lent him money which he had failed to repay and was now suing him. So Parsons overlooked the fact that the knockings began before the death of Fanny Lynes, and made no attempt to keep the revelations secret. In due course, Kent heard that he was being accused of murder by a "spirit", and came to the house in Cock Lane to hear it for himself. When the raps accused him of murder he shouted angrily, "Thou art a lying spirit."

The "ghost" became famous. But when a committee – including Dr Johnson – came to investigate, it preferred to remain silent convincing Johnson that it was a fraud. Then Kent decided to prosecute for libel. The burden of proof lay on Elizabeth's father, who was, for legal purposes, the accuser. There was another test and Elizabeth was told that if the ghost did not manifest itself this time, her mother and father would be thrown into prison. Naturally, she made sure something happened. But servants peering through a crack saw that she was making the raps with a wooden board. She was denounced as a fake. At the trial, Parsons was sentenced to two years in prison as well as to stand three times in the pillory. His wife received a year – a woman who had often "communicated" with the spirit received six months. Even the parson was fined £588 – a huge sum for those days. But when Parsons was standing in the pillory, the crowd was distinctly sympathetic and took up a collection for him – an unusual gesture in that age of cruelty, when crowds enjoyed pelting the malefactor in the pillory, sometimes even killing him. Regrettably, we know nothing of what happened to any of the protagonists after the trial. But it is very clear that the unfortunate Parsons family suffered a great injustice. Many witnesses testified earlier that it would have been impossible for Elizabeth to have faked the rapping noises.

The "Bell Witch"

One of America's most famous poltergeist cases occurred on the farm of a Tennessee farmer named John Bell – the case of the "Bell witch." It is also unusual – in fact, virtually unique – in that the poltergeist ended by causing the death of its victim, Bell, himself. Bell had nine children, one of whom (Betsy), was a girl of twelve. She was almost certainly the "focus." The disturbances began in 1817 with scratching noises from the walls, and occasional knocks. Then, invisible hands pulled bedclothes off the beds and there were choking noises that seemed to come from a human throat. Stones were thrown and furniture moved. The "spirit" frequently slapped Betsy and her cheek would redden after the sounds of the blow. It also pulled her hair. After about a year, the poltergeist developed a voice – a strange asthmatic croak. (Poltergeist voices seldom sound like human voices – it is as if the "entity" is having to master an unfamiliar medium.) It made remarks like, "I can't stand the smell of a nigger." After its manifestations Betsy was exhausted – she was obviously the source of its energy.

Then John Bell began to be attacked – his jaw

became stiff and his tongue swelled. The poltergeist, which had now developed a normal voice, identified itself as an Indian, then as a witch called Old Kate Batts. (It used several voices.) It also declared that it would torment John Bell until he died, which it then proceeded to do. It pulled off his shoes, hit him in the face and caused him to have violent physical convulsions. All this continued until, one day in 1820, he was found in a deep stupor. The "witch" claimed that she had given "old Jack" a dose of a medicine that would kill him. And when Bell did in fact die, the witch filled the house with shrieks of triumph. Then the disturbances abated.

One day in 1821, as the family was eating supper, there was a loud noise in the chimney and an object like a cannonball rolled out from the fireplace and turned into smoke. The witch's voice cried, "I am going and will be gone for seven years." But she stayed away for good.

One expert on poltergeists, Nandor Fodor, has suggested that the explanation of the Bell witch lies in an incestuous attack made on Betsy by her father, and that the poltergeist is a "personality fragment" that has somehow broken free of the rest of the personality. There is no real evidence for either of these claims.

Another famous American case took place in the home of the Revd Eliakim Phelps, in 1850. This poltergeist began by scattering furniture around and making curious dummies out of stuffed clothes. They were extremely lifelike and were constructed in a few minutes. Then the poltergeist entered the stone-

A seance, held by Mr Harry Hanks, to exorcise a poltergeist.

throwing stage (most disturbances seem to go through a number of definite phases), breaking 71 window-panes. Paper burst into flames and all kinds of objects were smashed. The 12-year-old boy, Harry, was snatched up into the air and on one occasion tied to a tree. His elder sister Anna, 16 was pinched and slapped. But when mother and children went off to Pennsylvania for the winter, the disturbances ceased.

Esther Cox

One of the most remarkable American cases of the nineteenth century was recorded in a book called *The Great Amherst Mystery* by Walter Hubbell, a stage magician who moved into the house of the Teed family in Amherst (Nova Scotia), in 1869, to investigate a poltergeist that concentrated its attention on an 18-year-old girl named Esther Cox. The disturbances had begun the previous year, when Esther's boyfriend, Bob MacNeal, had tried to order her into the woods at gunpoint, presumably to rape her. When interrupted, he fled and never returned. Soon after this, Esther and her sister Jane were kept awake by mouse-like rustling noises and a cardboard box that leapt into the air. Two nights later, Esther's body seemed to swell like a balloon but returned to normal after a sound like a thunderclap. Bedclothes were thrown around the room. Esther's pillow inflated like a balloon. In front of many witnesses, writing appeared on the wall saying, "Esther, you are mine to kill." Esther often complained of an "electric feeling" running through her body. When the poltergeist got into its stride, small fires broke out, objects flew around the room, furniture moved and Esther turned into a kind of human magnet, to which knives and other metal objects stuck firmly. Hubbell succeeded in communicating with the "spirits," who were able to prove their authenticity by telling him the number inside his watch and the date of coins in his pocket. When a barn burned down, Esther was accused of arson and sentenced to four months in prison. When she came out again the manifestations stopped.

Personality Fragments

The Society for Psychical Research was founded in 1882 to investigate "psychical phenomena" scientifically. One of its most influential members, Frank Podmore (author of a valuable two-volume history of Spiritualism), was firmly convinced the poltergeists were usually fakes, caused by stone-throwing children, although he *was* willing to admit that a well-known case at Durweston – on Viscount Portman's estate – was probably genuine. Podmore later had a lengthy correspondence with Andrew Lang, who found Podmore's skepticism too wholesale – Lang is generally conceded to have won this controversy.

In 1900, the famous criminologist, Cesare Lombroso, investigated a case of poltergeist-haunting in a wine shop in Turin. As Lombroso stood in the wine cellar, bottles gently rose from the shelves and exploded on the floor. At first Lombroso suspected that the proprietor's wife was the cause of the disturbances, but they continued while she was away. Lombroso's suspicions then focused on a 13-year-old waiter. When this boy was dismissed, the haunting stopped.

So it was fairly clear to the early investigators that poltergeist phenomena were connected, more often than not, with some particular person, usually an adolescent. (The word poltergeist was seldom used in the early days of psychical research, although it had been used to describe various cases by Mrs Catherine Crowe in her bestseller, *The Night Side of Nature* in 1848.) But it was not until the late 1940s that the "unconscious mind" theory became popular. Nandor Fodor put forward his theory that poltergeists are "personality fragments" in *The Journal of Clinical Psychopathology*, in 1945.

Frank Harvey's play, *The Poltergeist* had a successful West End run in 1946. It was based on a case that had taken place at Pitmilly House, Boarshill, near Fife, in which £50 worth of fire damage had been caused – Harvey transferred it to a Dartmoor vicarage. His play popularized the "unconscious mind" theory, which had first been put forward about 1930 by Dr Alfred Winterstein, in discussing the case of the Austrian medium Frieda Weisl. The latter's husband described how, when they were first married, ornaments would fly off the mantelpiece when she had an orgasm.

The Countess Zoe Wassilko-Serecki had reached similar conclusions when she examined a young Romanian girl named Eleanore Zugun, who was continually slapped and punched by a poltergeist – bitemarks that appeared on her were often damp with saliva. By the end of the 1940s, the "unconscious mind" theory was generally accepted by those psychical investigators who were willing to believe that the poltergeist was not a fraud. This theory was summarized by BBC investigator Brian Branston in his book *Beyond Belief* (1976), "I believe that, on the evidence, we may claim as a working hypothesis that poltergeist phenomena are produced unconsciously by an individual whose psyche is disturbed, that the disturbed psyche reacts on the oldest part of the brain, the brain stem, which by means unknown to science produced the commonly recognizable poltergeist phenomena. And these phenomena are the overt cry for help: as the poem says . . . . 'I was not . . . . waving but drowning.' "

Yet Branston's own theory has been contradicted by a case he has cited earlier in the chapter on poltergeists – one that took place at Northfleet in Kent. Branston records that "spooks so upset the various tenants that the house finally became empty. Previous tenants named Maxted had young children, and the usual poltergeist phenomena had taken place – mouse-like scratching noises, then the bedclothes pulled off the bed, ornaments disappearing and reappearing, and so on. When Mrs Maxted saw the ghost of a six-year-old girl they decided to move out. The next tenants had no children; they heard strange noises in the bedrooms and smelt an unpleasant, rotting smell, but it was only after a year that they woke up to find one end of the bed rising up into the air, while beside the bed stood a pinkish-orange phantom, partly transparent, of a woman with no head. They also moved out. But even when the house was empty the next door tenants were able to hear thumping noises, and were alarmed when their own bed began to vibrate." So here, it seems, is a case where the 'poltergeist' remained in the house throughout two tenancies, and stayed on when the house was empty."

I myself accepted the "unconscious mind" theory for many years. It seemed to me to explain, for example, the curious story of the Rosenheim poltergeist, the story of which I presented on BBC television in 1976.

The Rosenheim Poltergeist

In 1967 the office of a lawyer in Rosenheim, Bavaria, became the scene of a number of violent poltergeist disturbances. Light tubes shattered, pictures turned on the walls and a heavy filing cabinet was moved as if it weighed only a few pounds. Moreover, the telephone bill was enormous because hundreds of calls had apparently been made to the talking clock – more calls than were physically possible in the time available. The "poltergeist" was apparently getting straight through the relays. A well-known professor of parapsychology from Freiburg, Hans Bender, went to investigate the case and soon observed that the disturbances only took place when a young girl named Anne-Marie Schaberl was in the office. Anne-Marie was a country girl who was unhappy working in a town. Her family life had been difficult – her father was a strict disciplinarian – and she was mistrustful and tense. Bender took her back to his laboratory to try various tests for extrasensory perception and she showed remarkable telepathic abilities. And while Anne-Marie was in Freiburg, the disturbances in the office ceased. But they continued at the mill where she found work. When someone was killed in an accident, Anne-Marie was blamed and she left. Her fiancé broke off his engagement to her because she had such an extraordinary effect on the electronic scoring equipment at his favorite bowling alley. Finally, she married and had a child, and the manifestations ceased.

Anne-Marie had no suspicion that she was the cause of the disturbances in the lawyer's office; indeed when I met him during the course of the program, Professor Bender told me that one of the first rules of poltergeist investigation is not to tell the "disturbed adolescent" that he – or she – is the real cause of the disturbances, for it usually terrifies them.

The Black Monk

In 1980, I heard of a poltergeist haunting that was even more astonishing than the Rosenheim case. It had taken place in Pontefract in Yorkshire and I heard about it from a friend of the family concerned, who seemed to think that it might make a book, rather like the best-selling *Amityville Horror*. The poltergeist had, it seemed, wrecked practically every breakable item in the house and made such loud drumming noises at night that neighbors gathered in crowds to listen. But in this case, a number of people concerned had apparently also seen the poltergeist, which took the form of a monk dressed in black. The friend of the family who contacted me was interested in local history and told me that his researches had revealed that there had once been a gallows on the site of the house, and that a Cluniac monk had been hanged there for rape in the time of Henry VIII.

On May 6, 1822, the poet Shelley was walking on the terrace of a house near San Terenzo, in northern Italy, with his friend Edward Williams. They were staring at the Mediterranean in the moonlight, when suddenly Shelley grasped Williams by the arm and pointed. "There it is again." When his shock subsided, he explained that he had seen a naked child rise from the sea and clap its hands as it smiled at him – Shelley said it was Allegra, the dead daughter of their friend Lord Byron.

A few days later, a sailing boat was delivered to Shelley. It had been built to his order in Genoa and he had called it the *Don Juan* after Byron's poem. Shelley later changed its name to the *Ariel*.

Shelley told his wife, Mary, that he had met his own double – or doppelgänger – as he walked along the terrace. Moreover, the wife of Edward Williams (a woman of strong common sense), saw Shelley walk past the bedroom window that looked out on the terrace. A few minutes later, he walked past yet again – *but walking the same way*. She was puzzled, for Shelley would have had to return along the terrace in the other direction – unless he had leapt over the wall at the end, which was twenty feet high. She remarked, "Good God, has Shelley leapt over the wall? Where can he have gone?" Trelawny, another friend who was in the room said, "No, Shelley has not gone past." And indeed, he proved correct – Shelley had not been on the terrace that morning and was far off at the time she saw him.

A few days later, on Monday July 8, 1822, Shelley and Williams sailed on the *Ariel* for Lerici across the bay. A young man called Charles Vivian was also with them. They never returned. Two weeks later, their bodies were washed ashore and burned – the Italian authorities had ordered all bodies to be burned to avoid the plague.

On February 3, the following year, Mary Shelley was sitting reading when she heard her husband's voice calling to her – not a ghostly voice but Shelley's normal voice. She looked up, startled, and remembered that Shelley was dead.

The story sounded almost too good to be true. But before deciding to write about it, I asked a friend who lived in the area, Brian Marriner, to go and investigate. He wrote me a long letter in which he outlined the story of the haunting, and I was left in no doubt that this was a genuine case, not a hoax. The daughter of the family, Diane Pritchard, had been dragged upstairs by the throat by the "Black Monk" and thrown out of bed repeatedly. But the ghost also seemed to have a sense of humor. When Aunt Maude, a determined skeptic, came to see for herself, a jug of milk floated out of the refrigerator and poured itself over her head. Later, what looked like two enormous hands appeared around the door – they proved to be Aunt Maude's fur gloves. As the gloves floated into the bedroom, Mrs Pritchard asked indignantly, "Do you still think it's the kids doing it?" Aunt Maude burst into "Onward Christian Soldiers" and the gloves proceeded to conduct her singing, beating in time.

Having studied Brian Marriner's report on the case, I concluded that there was not enough material there for a full-length book, but it would make an admirable center-piece for a book on poltergeists, on which there is an immense amount of well-authenticated material. Poltergeist cases seem to be among the most frequent of paranormal events. I sketched out an outline of a history of poltergeist phenomena and submitted it to my publisher, who wrote back to say he liked the idea. Then, accompanied by my wife, I set out for Yorkshire to investigate for myself.

On our way to Pontefract, we stopped for a night at the Hayes Conference Center in Swanwick, Derbyshire, where I was to lecture at a conference on the paranormal. The following afternoon, just as we were about to leave, someone mentioned that Guy Playfair was due to arrive in half an hour. He and I had corresponded but had never met. So, although I was anxious to get on to Yorkshire, I decided to stay around for another half hour to introduce myself. It proved to be one of those fateful decisions that exercise an immeasurable influence on the future.

Guy, I knew, had spent some time in Rio de Janeiro, where he had joined the Brazilian equivalent of the Society for Psychical Research and studied the local version of black magic, *umbandal*. I knew his book, *The Indefinite Boundary*, a scientific study of the paranormal, and was impressed by its logic and detachment. I was just as impressed by Playfair himself, a quietly-spoken man whose modest utterances nevertheless carried total conviction. For half an hour or so we talked about ley lines, animal homing and telepathy. Then, just as it was time to leave, I told him I was writing a book on the poltergeist and asked his opinion. He frowned, hesitated, then said, "I think it's a kind of football." "Football!" (I wondered if I'd misheard him.) "A football of energy. When people get into conditions of tension, they exude a kind of energy – the kind of thing that happens to teenagers at puberty. Along come a couple of spirits, and they do what any group of schoolboys would do – they begin to kick it around, smashing windows and generally creating havoc. Then they get tired and leave it. In fact the football often explodes, and turns into a puddle of water."

"So you mean a poltergeist is actually a spirit?"

"That's right. I'm not saying there's not such a thing as spontaneous psychokinesis. But most poltergeists are spirits." And he advised me to read the French spiritualist, Allan Kardec.

I must admit that I found this notion hard to swallow. Ever since making the program on the Rosenheim case, I had taken it for granted that poltergeists are some kind of strange manifestation of the unconscious mind. I was not sure where the energy came from, but suspected that it was from the earth itself. I had seen a dowser standing above an underground spring, his fingers locked together and his hands pumping up and down so violently that the sweat poured down his face – he was obviously unable to stop himself while his hands were together. And at a dowsing conference, I had been introduced to an old lady who sometimes picked up a large fallen branch and used it as a dowsing rod. Suspended in one hand, it would swing from side-to-side like a huge voltmeter needle. It seemed to me highly likely that the energy used by the poltergeist flows from the earth via the right brain of the disturbed adolescent. And now Guy Playfair was advising me to abandon these carefully constructed theories and return to a view that sounded like crude medieval superstition.

The following afternoon we arrived at the home of Joe and Jean Pritchard in Pontefract. It was the typically neat home of an upper-working-class family. Their 19-year-old son, Phillip, was at home and during the course of the afternoon their daughter Diane came over with her husband to join us. These two had been the unconscious cause of the events that had caused a local sensation in 1966. I asked how the disturbances had begun. "With these pools of water on the kitchen floor." Joy and I looked at one another. "Can you describe their shape?" Mrs Pritchard shook her head. "They were just neat little pools – like overturning an ink bottle." This, according to Playfair, was a description of the pools of water created by the explosion of the "energy football". He said it was almost impossible to make them by pouring water on the floor – from a jug for example – because it splashes. These pools look as if a small cat has placed its behind close to the floor and urinated. I began to feel there might be something in his spirit theory after all.

Mrs Pritchard said that as fast as they mopped up the pools they reappeared elsewhere. But waterboard officials could find no leak. And when the tap was turned on, green foam rushed out. Then the button on the tea dispenser began to move in and out, covering the draining board with dry tea leaves; lights switched on and off and a plant-pot somehow found its way from the bottom to the top of the stairs.

The first set of manifestations occurred in 1966 and Phillip was obviously the focus since Diane was away on holiday at the time. Two days later, they ceased. But when they began again in 1968, Diane – now 14 – had become the focus. The ghost seldom paid a visit during the day, when she was at school. But in the evening the racket would start – usually a noise like a child beating a big drum – and ornaments would levitate across the room while the lights turned erratically on and off. Yet the poltergeist did not seem malicious – rather an infuriating practical joker. After a tremendous crash, all the contents of the china cabinet were found scattered around the sitting room, yet not one was even cracked. When the vicar came to try to exorcise the poltergeist and told the family that he thought their trouble was subsidence, a candlestick rose from the shelf and floated under his nose. The exorcism was unsuccessful.

Diane found it frightening, yet less so than might be expected. She always had a kind of inward notification when the pranks were about to start. Hurled violently out of bed with the mattress on top of her, she was unhurt. When the hall stand – made of heavy oak – floated through the air and pinned her down on the stairs (with a sewing machine on top of it for good measure), she was unable to move and the family were unable to budge it – yet she was not even bruised. When the ghost – whom they called "Mr Nobody" – hurled the grandfather clock downstairs so that it burst like a bomb, no one was anywhere near.

At a fairly late stage in the haunting, the ghost began to show itself. Jean and Joe Pritchard awakened one night to see a dim figure standing in the open doorway. Their next-door neighbor was standing at the sink when she felt someone standing behind her – it proved to be a tall figure in a monk's habit with a cowl over the head. It looked so solid and normal that she felt no alarm, then it vanished. Another neighbor, Rene Holden (who was a bit psychic), was in the Pritchards' sitting room when the lights went out. In the faint glow of the streetlamp that came through the curtains, she saw the lower half of a figure dressed in a long black garment.

The haunting was nearing its climax. One evening when the lights went out, Diane was heard to scream. The family rushed into the hall and found her being dragged up the stairs. The ghost seemed to have one hand on her cardigan, which was stretched out in front of her, and the other on her throat. As Phillip and Jean Pritchard grabbed her, the ghost let go and they all tumbled down the stairs. Diane's throat was covered with red finger-marks, yet "Mr Nobody" had not exerted enough pressure to hurt her. Soon after this, Jean Pritchard came downstairs to find the hall carpet soaked in water – on the wet surface there were huge footprints.

One day, Phillip and Diane were watching television when they both saw the "Black Monk" – or at least his shape – silhouetted on the other side of the frosted glass door that led to the dining room. As Phillip opened the door they saw his tall, black shape in the process of vanishing. It seemed to disappear into the kitchen floor. And that was the end of the Pontefract haunting. "Mr Nobody" disappeared and has not been heard from since.

I spent the whole of that Sunday afternoon listening to recordings of the poltergeist making violent banging noises, and questioning the family and neighbors. I also read the accounts contained in the local newspapers at the time. There could not be the slightest reasonable doubt that the haunting was genuine – there were too many witnesses.

Even if I had not met Guy Playfair, some of the features of the case would have puzzled me. This poltergeist behaved more like a ghost, and its connection with the former Cluniac monastery and the local gallows was fairly well established. In that case, the theory that it was really a kind of astral juvenile delinquent from Diane's unconscious mind seemed absurd. Besides, as Diane described her feelings as she was pulled upstairs by "Mr Nobody", I experienced a sudden total conviction that this was an independent entity, not a split-off fragment of her own psyche. When I left the Pritchards' house that afternoon, I had no doubt whatever that Guy Playfair was right – poltergeists are spirits.

It was an embarrassing admission to have to make. With the exception of Guy Playfair, there is probably not a single respectable parapsychologist in the world who will publicly admit the existence of spirits. Many will concede in private that they are inclined to accept the evidence for life after death, but in print even that admission would be regarded as a sign of weakness. Before that trip to Pontefract, I had been in basic agreement with them – it seemed totally unnecessary to assume the existence of spirits. Tom Lethbridge's "tape-recording" theory explained hauntings; the "unconscious" and the "information universe" combined to explain mysteries like telepathy, psychometry, even precognition. Spirits were totally irrelevant. Yet the Pontefract case left me in no doubt that the poltergeist was some local monk who died in a sudden and violent death, perhaps on the gallows, and who might or might not be aware that he was dead. And I must admit that it still causes me a kind of flash of protest to write such a sentence – the rationalist in me wants to say, "Oh come off it . . . ." Yet the evidence points clearly in that direction and it would be simple dishonesty not to admit it.

When I returned from Yorkshire, I took a deep breath and plunged into the annals of poltergeist activity with the aid of the library at the Society for Psychical Research and the College of Psychic Studies. The picture that now began to emerge made me aware of how far my preconceptions had caused me to impose an unnatural logic on the whole subject of the paranormal. It was not so much that the conceptions underlying my previous books *The Occult* and *Mysteries* were wrong, as that they were incomplete. And much of the evidence required to complete them had been staring me in the face from the beginning.

3

Spooks and Hobgoblins

The paranormal historian, Brian Inglis, has stated one of the most basic reasons for accepting the reality of ghosts – that every civilization in history has accepted them. There are hundreds of thousands of reported cases.

He might have gone further and pointed out that every civilization in history has believed in life after death. Modern western civilization is the first, so far, that has not taken life after death for granted.

This came about in the early nineteenth century as a result of the "enlightenment" of the previous century. The "Age of Reason" rejected witchcraft as a superstition, and the belief in "spirits" was the next to go.

Psychic Powers

In fact, every civilization has had its equivalent of *shamans*, witch doctors or mediums who have acted as intermediaries between the physical world and the world after death. But then, in the mid-eighteenth century, the great mystic, Emanuel Swedenborg, repeatedly showed the same ability. One of his contemporaries, Count Hopken, writes:

"Swedenborg was one day at a court reception. Her Majesty asked him about different things in the other life, and lastly, whether he had seen or talked with her brother, the Prince Royal of Prussia. He answered no. Her Majesty then requested him to ask after him, and give him her greeting, which Swedenborg promised to do. I doubt whether the Queen meant this seriously. At the next reception Swedenborg again appeared at court; and while the Queen was . . . . surrounded by her ladies of honour, he came boldly forward and approached Her Majesty . . . . Swedenborg not only greeted her from her brother, but also gave her his apologies for not having answered her last letter. He also wished to do so now through Swedenborg which he accordingly did. The Queen was greatly overcome and said, 'No one but God knows this secret.'"

In 1761, Mme de Marteville, the widow of the Dutch ambassador, asked Swedenborg for his help. A silversmith was demanding payment for a silver tea service, and she was certain her husband had paid for it before his death. However, she could not find the receipt. She asked Swedenborg if he could "contact" her husband. Swedenborg said he would try. A few days later he told Mme de Marteville that he had spoken to her husband, who said that the tea service *had* been paid for, seven months before his death, and that the receipt would be found in the bureau drawer. Mme de Marteville replied that the bureau in question had been thoroughly searched. Swedenborg then described a secret compartment in the bureau that contained some private correspondence and the receipt. Both receipt and correspondence were found where Swedenborg had described them.

In spite of the prevailing atmosphere of skepticism, many persons of intelligence were interested in the "occult." There was a remarkable man called Heinrich Jung, better known as Jung-Stilling, the son of a charcoal burner, who gradually rose to become a professor of economics, and a friend of the poet, Goethe.

Jung-Stilling himself possessed psychic faculties, and his *Theory of the Science of Spirits* (1808), is full of interesting examples of ghosts, apparitions, and the exercise of psychic powers. At that time, Franz Anton Mesmer had achieved fame in Paris with his theory of "animal magnetism." Mesmer believed that the vital fluid that gives us life is analogous to magnetism in metals. He thought that trees and water can be charged with animal magnetism, which would then cure people of various ailments. It was one of his disciples, the Marquis de Puységur, who accidentally discovered hypnosis when he was trying to "influence" a peasant called Victor Race, who was tied against a tree. Race went into a trance, to Puységur's great amazement, and was able to answer questions even though he was obviously asleep. Eventually, the words "hypnotism" and "mesmerism" became confused. But Jung-Stilling was fascinated by the various phenomena of "animal magnetism," which he felt to be a new scientific approach to the vital forces in man.

Jung-Stilling tells an interesting story of the kind of unknown powers that some human beings possess.

The wife of a sea captain had not heard from her husband for a long time, and went to see a neighbor who was reputed to possess unusual powers. After listening to her story, he asked her to excuse him and went into the next room. She waited and finally went and peeped through a crack in the door. The man was lying on a sofa, apparently asleep. Not long after, he came back to her and explained that her husband was not dead or ill, but that he had simply been prevented from writing to her by various difficulties. Her husband, he said, was at that moment in a coffee house in London and would very soon be home again. Not long after that, the husband returned home and verified that the clairvoyant's information had been totally correct. She took her husband along to see the man, and her husband immediately recognized him as someone he had seen in a coffee house in London.

This kind of thing convinced Jung-Stilling that man possesses some kind of immortal spirit or soul as well as his physical body, and he went on to create an interesting – if pseudo-scientific – theory about the human soul and its relation to magnetism, electricity and light. Jung-Stilling died in 1817, but his books remained immensely popular and were reprinted many times.

The Seeress of Prevorst

In 1826, a rich and eccentric doctor named Justinus Kerner heard about the case of a woman who often fell into a trance and saw invisible spirits. Her name was Friederike Hauffe and she was dying of a wasting disease. Her problems were apparently due to marriage. She had been married at the age of 19 to a cousin and had her first child, but immediately after that had fallen into depression. Evidently motherhood did not suit her. Every evening, she slipped into a trance in which she saw spirits of the dead. Kerner was told that she was able to predict the future.

He found that Friederike looked like a corpse, with yellow skin and very few teeth. Yet he was soon convinced that she possessed remarkable powers. When she claimed to be able to read with her stomach, he tested her by making her lie down with her eyes closed and laid books or documents on her bare stomach – she read them perfectly. She claimed that her spirit often left her body and hovered about it.

One day, when she came out of a trance, Friederike told Kerner that she was being haunted by an unpleasant man with a squint. From her description, Kerner recognized him as a man who had died a few years earlier. According to Friederike, the man was suffering from a guilty conscious. He had been involved in embezzling money and another man had been blamed. Now he wanted to clear the man's name for the sake of his widow. This could be done by means of a certain document which would be found in a chest. The spirit "showed" Friederike the room where the document was to be found, and she saw a man who was working there. Her description was so good that Kerner was able to identify him as a certain Judge Heyd. When Judge Heyd was told about Friederike's vision, he was astonished – he had been sitting in the room, in exactly the place described, on that particular day. And the chest containing the document had been open beside him on the table. He searched the chest, according to Friederike's instructions, and found the document that proved that the accused man had been wronged so that his widow was able to obtain recompense.

Freiderike told Kerner that we are surrounded by spirits all the time, but unable to see them. She, on the other hand, was able to see them and talk to them. In order to convince Kerner, Friederike persuaded one of the spirits to make rapping noises, to make gravel and ash fall from the air and to make a stool float up into the air. Kerner watched with amazement as the stool gently rose up, then floated to the floor again.

Kerner had heard about a house where the ghost of an old man was frightening the inhabitants. He brought one of them to see Friederike – the seeress went into a trance and explained that the ghost was that of a man called Bellon who was an "earth-bound spirit," as a result of defrauding two orphans. Kerner made inquiries, but no one had ever heard of a man called Bellon. But since the ghost claimed that he had been the *burgomeister* (mayor), it seemed probable that some record existed. Kerner asked the present mayor to check the legal documents and soon found that a man called Bellon *had* been *burgomeister*, as well as director of the local orphanage. After "confessing" to Friederike, the spirit of Bellon ceased to haunt the house.

While Friederike was in Kerner's house, there were

constant poltergeist phenomena – knocks and raps, noises like the rattling of chains, gravel thrown through the window, and a knitting needle that flew through the air and landed in a glass of water. When Friederike was visited by a spirit one night, her sister heard her say, "Open it yourself," then saw a book on the table open itself. A poltergeist tugged her boots off her feet, as she lay on the bed, and threw a lampshade across the room. In the Kerners' bedroom, a table was thrown across the room. The poltergeist threw a stool at a maidservant who went into Friederike's room where she lay asleep.

Friederike also produced what would later be called "spirit teachings," an amazingly complex system of philosophy in which man is described as consisting of body, soul and spirit, and of being surrounded by a nerve aura which carries on the vital processes. She spoke about various cycles in human existence – life cycles (or circles and sun cycles), corresponding to various spiritual conditions. She also described a remarkable universal language from ancient times said to be the "language of the inner life."

All these activities exhausted Friederike, and she died in 1829 at the age of 28. In the year she died, Kerner wrote a book about her called *The Seeress of Prevorst*, which created a sensation.

Possession

Kerner also investigated another girl who was tormented by "spirits." The girl, who was a peasant, lived in a house in Orlach, near Stuttgart. She had been persecuted by "spirits" from the age of 20 – obviously the "focus" of poltergeist phenomena. Furniture was moved around and there were even outbreaks of fire. Then the girl saw two ghosts, one of a nun dressed in white, the other of a monk dressed in black. The nun claimed that she had been smuggled into the monastery disguised as a cook and had two children by the monk, both of whom he had killed at birth. He had also murdered three monks during the four year period that she had been with him. When he suspected that she was about to betray him, he killed her too. After this, the monk also spoke to the possessed girl, saying that he was the son of a nobleman, and that as the abbot at the monastery of Orlach he had seduced a number of nuns and killed the children they bore. He confessed to killing the monks and throwing the bodies into a hole in the wall.

It became clear that the cottage had been built on the site of the monastery, and the white nun told the girl that her sufferings would cease only if her parents agreed to the cottage's demolition. By this time, they were so desperate that they agreed. On March 5, 1833, the house was finally demolished. Most of the walls were made of mud but one corner was constructed of limestone, obviously part of the monastery. When this was pulled down, they found underneath an empty well containing a number of human bones, including those of children. The girl's possession ceased immediately.

Silver Belle — the medium's "guide" — dramatically emerges.

Spirit Guides

In 1839, another doctor – this time of philosophy –
produced another account of a case that bears some
similarity to Friederike Hauffe. It was called *The
Guardian Spirit* (*Die Schutzgeister*), and its author,
Dr Heinrich Verner, conceals the girl's identity under
the initials R.O.

Like Friederike, R.O. had been subject to all kinds of
illnesses, then, at a certain point, found herself
haunted by spirits. One day the girl fell into a trance
and from then on she was able to do so at will, and to
supply Verner with all kinds of information obtained
"clairvoyantly." She had a "guardian spirit" (of the
title) called Albert, who seems to have acted rather like
the "spirit guide" of later mediums. And the spirit who
caused her so much trouble was – again – a wicked
monk. One day, when the girl claimed that the wicked
monk was present in the room, Verner was puzzled to
hear an odd sound like a cup rattling on a saucer – R. O.
said that it was the monk who was producing the
noise. Another day, Verner was startled to hear a loud
crash from an empty room and found that two large
flowerpots had been hurled to the floor, so there was
earth all over the room. One of the curtains had been
twisted around a bird-cage. Later that day, Verner went
to call on R. O. who went into a trance and then told
Verner that the black monk had been responsible for
hurling down the flowerpots (Verner had not mentioned this to her). Albert, apparently, had thrown him
out of the house.

R. O. also showed clairvoyant powers. Once she woke from a trance and told him that she had seen herself driving in a green-lacquered chaise. At that time, Verner was considering buying a chaise and expected an answer in about a week. R. O. told him that he would hear much sooner than that – in fact, the following afternoon. She also went on to describe the chaise in some detail. The following afternoon, Verner received a message about the chaise and discovered that the girl was right in every detail.

One of her most dramatic pieces of clairvoyance concerned her younger sister, Emily. One day, in a trance, she cried out, "Albert, help me! Emily's falling down into the street." Then after a short period, she said, "Thank God, help has already come." Asked what had happened, she explained that her little sister had been leaning out of a top-storey window, trying to grab a rope suspended from a winch, when she had overbalanced and been unable to get back in. Her father had entered the room and pulled her back. Verner later asked her father if anything strange had happened that day. He replied that he had been sitting in his office when he had felt uneasy and hurried home. As he went into the room upstairs, he found his daughter leaning out of the window unable to get back in and had pulled her back by her dress. R. O. said that it was her "guardian spirit" Albert who had made her father feel uneasy.

The Seeress of Prevorst was read by an Edinburgh housewife – and novelist – named Catherine Crowe, who became fascinated by it and translated it into English. She then went on to put together her own compilation of stories – most of which she collected at first hand. *The Night Side of Nature* came out in 1846 and became an immediate bestseller – it was still in print, and on most railway bookstores, after the turn of the century.

Mrs Crowe is attempting to decide, in the book, whether there is enough evidence to prove that man survives the death of his body. And her first step in this direction was to try to show that man possesses powers that cannot be explained by science. She quotes Jung-Stilling's story about the sea captain's wife and the psychic who was able to tell her that her husband was in a coffee house in London. She also tells stories like the following:

"Another friend lately dreamt, one Thursday night, that he saw an acquaintance of his thrown from his horse, and that he was lying on the ground with the blood streaming from his face, and was much cut. He mentioned his dream in the morning, and being an entire disbeliever in such phenomena, he was unable to account for the impression it made on his mind. This was so strong that, on Saturday, he could not forbear calling at his friend's house, who he was told was in bed having been thrown from his horse on the previous day, and much injured about the face."

Later investigators have accused Mrs Crowe of being gullible but this is hardly borne out by the book itself. For example, her account of the haunting of a place called Willington Mill, near Newcastle, shows that, in going directly to the people involved, she was already anticipating the methods of the "Society for Psychical Research."

Hauntings

The haunted house was a millhouse – it had been built only 40 years earlier, in 1800. The newly-built Newcastle and Shields railway passed overhead on a viaduct. In June 1840, news reached the outside world that the Proctor family – who were Quakers – had been disturbed by knocking noises and had seen some unpleasant things. A surgeon named Edward Drury, who practised in Sunderland, heard about the haunting from a local farmer. Dr Drury was skeptical about such matters. Nevertheless, he had been fascinated by the account of a famous poltergeist haunting at Epworth, at the rectory of the Revd Samuel Wesley, grandfather of the founder of Methodism. This spook, known as "Old Jeffry", had banged and groaned around the rectory for two months in 1716. There were sounds of heavy breathing, breaking glass, footsteps, and various unidentifiable noises. The Revd Samuel noticed that the disturbances seemed in some way connected with his 19-year-old daughter Hetty, who trembled in her sleep before the sounds began. The scientist Joseph Priestley had investigated the case and decided it was a hoax. Dr Drury was inclined to agree with him, so when he heard of the "haunting" of Willington Mill, he wrote to its owner (Joshua Proctor), offering to "unravel the mystery" (that is, expose the hoaxer). Mr Proctor replied politely, saying that he and his family were going away on a visit on the date Mr Drury had suggested – one of his employees was going to act as caretaker while they were away. Nevertheless, if Drury wanted to come and stay overnight, he was welcome.

Dr Drury decided to take a friend along for moral support. He also took a brace of pistols, intending to allow one of them to fall on the floor as if by accident, to deter any practical joker. But when he arrived, he found that Joshua Proctor had returned – alone – from his holiday and Mr Proctor was so obviously an honest man that Drury decided the "accident" was unnecessary.

What happened to Edward Drury that night convinced him completely of the reality of the supernatural. It also gave him a temporary breakdown in health. He seems to have been too shattered to describe what he had seen immediately afterwards, but he promised to write Mr Proctor a letter with a full account. This letter was written on July 13, 1840, ten days after his night in the haunted millhouse.

He arrived with his friend, T. Hudson, and was made welcome by Mr Proctor who showed him over the house. At 11.00 p.m., Dr Drury and Mr Hudson settled down on the third-storey landing outside the "haunted room." (Although he says he "expected to account for any noises that he might hear in a philosophical manner," he presumably decided that discretion was the better part of valor.) About an hour later, they heard pattering noises "as if a number of people were pattering with their bare feet." Then there was a knocking sound from the floorboards at their feet, as if someone was rapping with his knuckles. After this, they heard a "hollow cough" from the haunted room but seem to have decided not to investigate. Then they heard a rustling noise, as if someone was coming upstairs.

At 12.45 a.m., feeling cold, Dr Drury said he thought he would retire to bed. Mr Hudson said he intended to stay up until dawn. Drury looked at his watch and noted the time. As he looked up, he saw a closet door open and "the figure of a female, attired in grayish garments, with the head inclining downwards, and one hand pressed upon the chest, as if in pain" walking towards him. Mr Hudson was fast asleep but was awakened by Drury's "awful yell." Drury rushed at the figure, "but instead of grasping it, I fell upon my friend, and I recollected nothing distinctly for nearly three hours afterwards. I have since learnt that I was carried downstairs in an agony of fear and terror."

Mrs Crowe not only publishes the full correspondence between Dr Drury and Joshua Proctor, but an account by a local historian, another by the owner of a local journal, and descriptions by four other people who had seen the ghost. In fact, there seemed to be more than one – there was also a man in a surplice who glided across a second-floor room at a distance of a few feet from the floor. The local historian adds to his account the information that Mr Proctor has recently discovered an old book that states that similar hauntings had taken place in an older house that had been built on the same spot, 200 years before. Mrs Crowe ends her account by mentioning that Mr Proctor has now decided to leave the house, and turn it into "small tenements" for his work people.

What makes this report so interesting is that the

case resembles in so many respects the "haunting" that would occur eight years later in Hydesville, New York, and which launched the Spiritualist movement of the nineteenth century. In Willington, as in Hydesville, there was a mixture of "poltergeist" phenomena and the more conventional type of haunting. If Dr Drury had shown the same kind of courage and curiosity shown later by Mrs Margaret Fox at Hydesville, it seems highly probably that the Spiritualist movement would have been launched ten years earlier in England.

The Hydesville affair began on March 31, 1848, in a wooden frame house inhabited by a Methodist farmer named James D. Fox, his wife Margaret, and their two daughters, Margaretta (aged 14), and Kate (aged 12). Hydesville is a small township not far from Rochester, New York. James Fox had moved into the house the previous December. A previous tenant, Michael Weekman, had been disturbed by various loud knocks for which he could find no cause.

The Fox family was also kept awake by various banging noises in the last days of March 1848, but since it was a windy month, they were not unduly disturbed. On Friday, March 31, the family decided to retire early to make up for lost sleep. Mr Fox went round the house checking the shutters and sashes. The children observed that when he shook the sashes, to see how loose they were, banging noises seemed to reply like an echo.

The whole family slept in two beds in the same room. Just before the parents came to bed, the rapping noises started again. Kate said cheekily "Mr Splitfoot, do as I do," and began snapping her fingers. To the amazement of the girls, the raps imitated her. Remembering that the next day would be April 1st, the children decided that someone was playing a joke. In her account of what happened, Mrs Fox wrote,

"I then thought I could put a test that no one in the place could answer. I asked the noise to rap my different children's ages, successively. Instantly, each one of my children's ages was given correctly, pausing between them sufficiently long to individualize them until the seventh [child], at which a longer pause was made, and then three more emphatic little raps were given corresponding to the age of the little one that died . . . ."

Now rather frightened – this was evidently no joke – Mrs Fox asked if it was a human being who was making the raps – there was no reply. "Is it a spirit? If it is, make two raps." Two thunderous bangs followed, so loud that the house shook. She asked if it was an "injured spirit," and again the bangs shook the house. Further questioning revealed that the knocker was a man who had died at the age of 31, that he had been murdered in the house and that he had a wife and five children. Mrs Fox asked if the spirit had any objection to her calling in the neighbors – the raps replied "No."

The Foxes summoned in about 14 neighbors. One of these was a man called William Duesler, who assured his own wife that the whole thing was ridiculous and that there could be nothing mysterious about the noises. When he got there, some of the neighbors were too nervous to go into the bedroom but Duesler was not worried. He went and sat on the bed, and was astonished when Mrs Fox's questions were answered with a rapping noise that made the bed vibrate. (Later writers were to insist that the two children made all the noises by cracking their joints – but is is hard to see how the cracking of joints could make the house shake and cause a bed to vibrate.)

Duesler took up the questioning of the "spirit." By a code of knocks, he established that the entity was a man who had been murdered in the house, a pedlar named Charles B. Rosma, who had been attacked for the $500 he carried. The murder had taken place five years earlier, and had been committed by the man who was then the tenant of the house – a Mr Bell. A maid named Lucretia Pulver later confirmed that a pedlar *had* spent the night in the house and that she had been sent home – when she returned the next day, the pedlar had gone.

As news of these amazing occurrences spread throughout the community, hundreds of people came to the house. On Sunday, April 2, Duesler learned from the murdered man that his body had been buried in the cellar. This seemed to offer a method of verification and James Fox and his neighbors took shovels to the cellar – which had an earth floor – and proceeded to dig. At a depth of three feet they encountered water and abandoned the attempt. But in July, when the water had gone down, they dug again and at a depth of five feet found a plank – underneath this, in quicklime, there was some human hair and a few bones.

Mr Bell, on hearing that he had been accused of

murder by a ghost, indignantly denied it and produced a testimonial to his good character from his new neighbors in Lyon, New York. The spirit had already prophesied that the murderer would never be brought to justice.

In his account of the case in *Modern Spiritualism*, the skeptical Frank Podmore comments, "No corroborative evidence of the supposed murder, or even of the existence of the man supposed to have been murdered, was ever obtained." This was written in 1902. Two years later, in November 1904, a wall in the cellar of the Fox house collapsed, revealing another wall behind it. Digging between the two walls uncovered a skeleton and a pedlar's tin box. It looked as if someone had dug up the body from its original grave and interred it next to the wall, then built another wall to confuse searchers.

In those days, immediately after the first manifestations, a committee was set up to collect the statements of witnesses. Not all the investigators were convinced that the sounds had a supernatural origin, but no one suggested that the Fox family could be responsible. With the family all together in the same room, it was obviously impossible that either the parents or the children could be causing the bangs.

What everyone soon noticed was that nothing happened unless the children were in the house – particularly Kate. A committee of skeptical Rochester citizens came to the house to investigate – they agreed that Margaret was certainly not responsible. A second then a third investigation produced the same result. The children were stripped and searched to see if they had some mechanical device for producing the sounds – there was nothing. They were made to stand on pillows with their ankles tied but still the raps occurred.

The children were separated – Kate was sent to stay with her elder sister, Leah, in Rochester, and Margaretta with her brother David in Auburn. The "spirits" followed them both. Rapping noises were heard and people felt themselves touched by invisible hands. In Leah's house, a lodger called Calvin Brown took a mildly satirical attitude towards the spirit and it began to persecute him, throwing things at him. Mrs Fox's cap was pulled off and the comb pulled out of her hair. When members of the family knelt to pray, pins were jabbed into them. In brother David's boarding house, similar things were happening. It was clear that the murdered pedlar was not responsible for all this – he was back in the Hydesville house, making terrifying gurgling noises and sounds like a body being dragged across the floor. Mrs Fox's hair turned white. One spirit who communicated with Kate claimed to be a dead relative named Jacob Smith. Sister Leah Fish discovered that she could also communicate with the spirits and began producing messages. One 16-year-old girl named Harriet Bebee, who visited the house in Auburn and witnessed the rapping noises, returned to her home miles away and found that the noises had followed her.

The Fox family moved to Rochester, but the manifestations continued. Sometimes the bangs were so loud that they could be heard miles away. Poltergeists had apparently taken over from the original "injured spirit." One day, a visitor named Isaac Post started asking the spirit questions and was answered by a thunderous barrage of knocks. Then, by means of an alphabetical code, the "spirit" spelled out a message – "Dear friends, you must proclaim this truth to the world. This is the dawning of a new era; you must not try to conceal it any longer. God will protect you and good spirits will watch over you." And now began a series of manifestations that were to become typical of "spiritualism." Tables moved and rapped with their legs, musical instruments were played by unseen fingers, objects moved round the room. The "spirits" intimated that they would prefer to manifest themselves in the dark – which confirmed the skeptics in their opinion. But other believers decided it was time to put the "spirit's" injunction into operation and "proclaim this truth to the world." On November 14, 1849, the first Spiritualist meeting took place in the Corinthian hall in Rochester. One writer commented, "Were we to draw an inference from the number of cases of reported visitations from the invisible world that have been made public of late, we might be led to imagine that the days of supernatural agency were about to recommence, and that ghosts and hobgoblins were about to resume their sway over the fears of mankind."

For 1850, that was a remarkably perceptive observation. Whether it was merely due to improved communications and the increase in the number of newspapers, it *does* seem clear that there was an apparent increase in ghostly manifestations at about this period. In retrospect, it looks as if the "spirits" had decided that the time had come to make themselves noticed. Of course, there had been such manifestations for centuries – the Elizabethan astrologer, Dr John Dee, devoted a large book to an account of his communications with "spirits" through the agency of a "scryer" (or, as they later came to be called, medium) called Edward Kelley. Cases like the Epworth poltergeist, the Stockwell poltergeist (described by Mrs Crowe), the Cock Lane ghost and the phantom drummer of Tedworth had aroused widespread excitement and been the subject of contemporary pamphlets. In 1847, a young American shoemaker named Andrew Jackson Davis was placed under hypnosis and wrote an extraordinary and erudite work called *The Principles of Nature*, which subsequently became a literary sensation. In this remarkable book, Davis prophesies that "the truth about spirits will ere long present itself in the form of a living demonstration, and the world will hail with delight the ushering in of that era when the interiors of men will be opened." Within four years of its publication, Spiritualism had spread across America and was sweeping Europe.

For whatever reason, the Fox sisters began a Spiritualist explosion. People discovered that all they had to do was to sit in a darkened room, preferably with a "medium" (or intermediary) present – someone who had already established a communication with the spirits – and the manifestations would usually follow immediately. No apparatus was required, except possibly a few musical instruments. In the Rochester area, more than 100 "mediums" appeared in the year 1850.

In Buffalo, New York, two brothers and a sister named Davenport attended a seance at which the Fox sisters produced their manifestations, and decided to try it themselves – in fact, inexplicable raps and bangs had sounded in their home in the year 1846, two years before the Hydesville manifestations. When Ira, William and Elizabeth Davenport sat in a darkened room with their hands on a tabletop, the table began to move, raps were heard all over the room, and when Ira picked up a pencil his hand began to write automatically. A few nights later, with witnesses present, all three children were seen to levitate into the air. At their fifth "seance," Ira was instructed – by means of raps – to fire a pistol in the corner of the room. As it exploded, it was taken from his hand, and by the light of the flash, a figure of a man was seen holding it. He vanished a moment later and the pistol fell to the floor. The man introduced himself – through the code of raps – as John King. He was one of the first examples of a "control" (or master of ceremonies), who acted as intermediary between the medium and the "spirits." John King was soon taking over the brothers directly and speaking through their mouths. The Davenport brothers went on to become even more famous than the Fox sisters.

In Dover, Ohio, a well-to-do farmer named Jonathan Koons discovered his own talents as a "medium" by sitting in a dark room and going into a trance. The "spirits" who spoke through him told him that all his eight children were gifted "mediums." They instructed him to build a special house made of logs, 16 feet by 12 feet, to be used exclusively for spiritualist

On February 8, 1935, a market gardener named John Puckering (who lived in Arley, Warwickshire), died during the course of an operation. Although the heart had stopped beating for nearly five minutes, the surgeon opened his chest and massaged his heart until Puckering revived. He said that he had made the incision more from a sense of duty than from any hope that he would succeed.

Puckering was not at all grateful. "What I saw during my brief spell of death makes me regret that I ever came back." He said that he had found himself surrounded by thousands of happy people and when he recognized his wife – who had been dead for a year – among them, he realized that he was among the dead. Now back on earth, he was disappointed to be alive again but commented, "The grave has no terrors for me now. I realize that earthly life is just a training ground for something fuller and better."

activities. There were large numbers of musical instruments – drums, triangles, tambourines, a banjo, an accordion, a harp, a guitar and so on. The room was dimly lit by sheets of wet paper smeared with phosphorus. When the "mediums" – usually Koons and his 18-year-old son, Nahum – were seated at a small table (with the audience on benches), Koons would play the violin and the spirits would soon join in, producing the effect of a full orchestra. Witnesses also speak of a heavenly choir joining in. The racket was impressive and could be heard a mile away. A voice

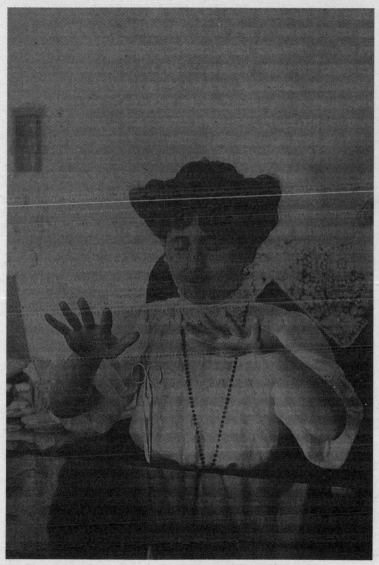

Levitation of scissors by Stanislawa Tomczyk.

would then deliver a homily, using a speaking trumpet, which floated in the air. A spirit hand floated round the room, touching people and shaking their hands. People came from all over the county to witness these marvels and the spirits impressed everyone by producing information about strangers that none of the audience could have known.

This was, in fact, one of the most convincing things about the "spirits" – they seemed to have access to all kinds of information. In Boston, the wife of a newspaper editor, Mrs W. R. Hayden, startled the wife of the English mathematician, Augustus de Morgan, by giving her detailed messages from dead friends about whom she could not possibly have known. The result was that Mrs de Morgan invited her to England, where she held seances under "test conditions" in the de Morgans' home. She was ridiculed by the English newspapers, who were convinced that this latest American craze must be based on fraud and deception (which the British were too sensible to swallow), but she convinced most of those who actually saw her. And respectable members of the British middle classes who tried "table-turning" to while away the long evenings were amazed to discover that it actually worked. One journalist wrote a few years later, "In those days you were invited to 'Tea and Table Moving' as a new excitement, and made to revolve with the family like mad around articles of furniture." Even Queen Victoria and Prince Albert tried it at Osborne, and the table moved so convincingly that the Queen had no doubt whatever that there was no trickery involved – she decided that the answer must lie in some form of electricity or magnetism.

The French were more than prepared to adopt this new form of entertainment, for half a century of controversy about Mesmer – who had taught that healing, clairvoyance and other such mysteries were due to a mysterious force called "animal magnetism" – had accustomed them to strange phenomena. By 1851, table-turning had become the latest craze and the spirits soon made a highly influential convert. He was a 50-year-old educationalist named Denizard-Hyppolyte-Leon Rivail, who was to become famous under the name "Allan Kardec." Rivail had been a pupil of the celebrated educator Pestalozzi, and he had opened his own school at the age of 24. He had written popular books on arithmetic, grammar, spelling, how to calculate in your head and educational reform, and given immensely successful courses of free lectures in astronomy, chemistry, physics and anatomy. He was also an enthusiastic student of phrenology and "animal magnetism."

It was in May 1855 that Rivail attended a hypnotic session with a certain Mme Roger, who was placed in a trance by her "magnetiser," M. Fortier, and was able to read minds and perform other puzzling feats. There Rivail met Mme Plainemaison, who told him that even stranger phenomena were taking place regularly at her house in the Rue Grange-Bateliere. Rivail agreed to go and was amazed by what he saw. The tables did more than merely "turn" – they also jumped and ran about the room. The disciple of Mesmer felt that these phenomena challenged the powers of reason to which he had devoted his life, and he determined to try to get to the bottom of it. At Mme Plainemaison's home, he met a man named Baudin, who told him that his two daughters practised automatic writing. The young ladies seem to have discovered their powers accidentally, in the course of entertaining their friends with table-turning; they were, says one commentator, "of a worldly and frivolous disposition." This did not deter the serious-minded Rivail, who proceeded to ask the table major philosophical questions. Asked if mankind would ever understand the first principles of the universe, it replied, "No. There are things that cannot be understood by man in this world." When Rivail asked if matter had always existed, the table replied (perhaps a trifle wearily), "God only knows."

It was obvious to Rivail that the entities who were communicating were genuine spirits, not the unconscious minds of the young ladies. (Even in those days, the concept of the unconscious was accepted.) In fact, the communicators identified themselves as "spirits of genii," and said that some of them (but not all) had been the spirits of those who had been alive on earth.

With excitement, Rivail realized that this material had an impressive inner-consistency, and that the total pattern revealed a philosophical scheme that embraced the whole universe. Other friends who had been collecting "automatic scripts" – including the playwright Sardou – handed over their own material to Rivail (more than fifty notebooks.) And Rivail was told to bring all this material together into a book which should be called *The Spirits' Book*. The spirits even gave Rivail the pseudonym under which he should publish the work – "Allan Kardec." Both of these names – according to the spirits – were names he had borne in previous incarnations.

The message of *The Spirits' Book* is easily summarized. Man is a fourfold being, made up of body, "vital principle" (aura), intelligent soul and spiritual soul – the divisions we have already encountered in the *Seeress of Prevorst*. Spirits are intelligent beings who constitute the "population of the universe." Man is a spirit enclosed in a physical body. The destiny of all spirits is to evolve towards perfection. There are three basic categories of spirit – the "low spirits," who are trapped in materiality, the "second degree spirits," whose moral nature has evolved to the point where they experience only a desire for good, and the "perfect spirits," who have reached the peak of their evolution. The "low spirits" range from evil spirits who are activated by malice, to mere "boisterous spirits" who enjoy getting into mischief. These latter are also known as poltergeists. After death, a spirit spends some time in the spirit world and is then reincarnated on earth or some other world. The purpose of earthly life is to enable the spirit to evolve. To some extent, the spirit is able to choose the trials it will undergo in its next life. (This means that it is pointless to bemoan our lot since we have chosen it ourselves.)

The Spirits' Book appeared in 1856, and created a sensation. Kardec became the founder-figure of the French spiritualist movement and his works attained immense influence. But he died of a heart attack (only thirteen years after the book was published) at the age of 65, and his influence was soon being widely questioned by the movement. Rivail was totally committed to the doctrine of reincarnation, the slow perfection of the spirit through a series of rebirths, which can be traced back to ancient India. But most of the "spirits" who spoke through mediums at seances had nothing to say about reincarnation. So Rivail was inclined to be critical about the trance "mediums" and their followers denounced Rivail as a dogmatic old man. After Rivail's death, his influence waned and within a few years he was half-forgotten.

Now in Paris, in 1860, there was a particularly violent poltergeist in the Rue des Noyers – it smashed every window in the building, hurled all kinds of objects around the place (including many which the occupants had never seen before), and finally drove the unfortunate people out of the house. Rivail decided to try to find out what exactly had happened. His medium's "control" (the spirit who acts as master of ceremonies), explained that the disturbances were the work of a mischievous spirit. And, at the request of the control (a spirit called Saint Louis), the poltergeist of the Rue des Noyers was summoned. He appeared to be in a bad temper and asked irritably, "Why do you call me? Do you want to have some stones thrown at you?" Rivail now asked the spirit, "Was there anyone in the Rue des Noyers who helped you play tricks on the inmates?" "Certainly," replied the spirit, "it had an excellent 'instrument.'" It added, "For I am merry and like to amuse myself sometimes." Who was it? Rivail asked. "A maidservant."

"Was she unaware you were making use of her?"

"Oh yes, poor girl – she was the most frightened of them all."

Rivail asked how the spirit managed to throw various objects about the place and received the interesting answer, "I helped myself through the electric nature of the girl, joined to my own . . . . we were able to transport the objects between us."

Rivail asked the spirit who it was. It replied that it had been dead about 50 years, and had been a rag-and-bone-man. People used to make fun of him because he drank too much and this was why he decided to play tricks on the inhabitants of the Rue des Noyers. He indignantly denied that he had done these things out of malice – it was merely his way of amusing himself.

This spirit seems to belong to a class described in *The Spirits' Book*, "They are ignorant, mischievous, unreasonable, and addicted to mockery. They meddle with everything and reply to every question without paying attention to the truth."

So, according to Kardec, poltergeists are mischievous spirits who draw their energy from certain "vulnerable" human beings.

In all but one respect, Kardec's "spirit teaching" agreed basically with those of most other spiritualists since Swedenborg. But that one aspect, reincarnation, was to prove a source of severe contention within the French spiritualist movement. *The Spirits' Book* had already been anticipated by a work called *Arcanes de la vie future devoilée* – (*Secrets of the Future Life Unveiled*), by Alphonse Cahagnet, published in 1848 (and a second and third volume later.) Cahagnet was a cabinet maker who had become fascinated by hypnotism in his mid-30s. He placed various subjects in a hypnotic trance – the most impressive being a woman called Adele Maginot – and recorded what they told him of life after death. Adele was so remarkable because her messages from the dead (and sometimes from living people who had disappeared), were so full of convincing evidence. Cahagnet started a journal called *The Spiritualist Magnetiser*, and this was later transformed into *The Spiritualist Revue*, edited by Z. Pierart. But Cahagnet, who was a follower of Swedenborg, did not believe in reincarnation. And the French spiritualist movement was soon split by a bitter war of words between the followers of Cahagnet and the followers of Kardec. Kardec was critical of trance mediums – like Adele – because they had nothing to say about reincarnation, and Cahagnet and his followers regarded automatic writing with suspicion and disdain. But while Kardec died in 1869, Cahagnet lived and flourished until 1885, publishing many more influential books. So it was Kardec's version of spiritualism that gradually faded away as the movement became increasingly powerful. It was only in Brazil – a country whose witch-doctors frequently called on the spirits for magical aid – that Kardec's version of spiritualism took root and where it still flourishes today as one of the country's major religions.

It may be as well, at this point, to pause and ask the question, "what does it all mean?" There is something about "spiritualism" that is peculiarly irritating. It is one thing to accept that some people possess strange powers of clairvoyance, and quite another to swallow

Miss Cummins, a leading spiritualist automatic writer of the 1920s, writes in a light trance, holding her head on her hand.

"spirit teachings" that sound like the ramblings of an uninspired Sunday school teacher. It is not that the doctrines of Swedenborg or Kardec are in themselves unacceptable. The notion that man possesses a "vital body," an "astral body" and an "ego-body" seems reasonable enough. Some may even learn, through self-observation, to distinguish between the promptings of the "low self" and the detached observations of some higher part of us that looks down ironically on our sufferings and humiliations. But when Kardec tells us that God created spirits and then set them the task of evolving towards perfection, it sounds boringly abstract. *Why* did God bother to create spirits in the first place? And surely spirits ought to have something better to do than to communicate with their living relatives through "mediums" and deliver anti-climactic messages about the joys of the afterlife and the trivial problems of the living? If we compare the revelations of spiritualism with those of science or philosophy, or the visions of the great mystics, they seem oddly banal. . . .

This explains why spiritualism aroused such instant hostility among scientists and philosophers. Spiritualism was like a volcanic explosion of belief – the scientists replied with a blast of skepticism that was like cold water. And the combination of boiling lava and cold water produced an enormous cloud of steam that obscured everything. It was not that most scientists disbelieved the evidence – they refused even to look at it. T. H. Huxley expressed the general feeling when he remarked, "It may all be true, for anything that I know to the contrary, but really I cannot get up interest in the subject."

4

Ghost Hunters

In the 1860s, one of the most famous teachers at Cambridge was Professor Henry Sidgwick of Trinity College. Like so many Victorians, he was tormented by religious doubts and by the question of whether human life makes any sense. By his students, he was regarded as one of the great wise men of the age – a kind of Socrates. These included Arthur Balfour (future prime minister), Edmund Gurney (heir to a Quaker fortune), and Frederic Myers (the son of a clergyman.) One evening in December 1869, Myers paid a visit to his old master and they went for a walk under the stars. There they talked about the "riddle of the universe," and Myers asked whether, since science and philosophy had failed to solve it, there might be just a chance that the answer might lie in all the new evidence for ghosts and spirits.

It took a long time for the idea to come to fruition, but the final result was the foundation of the Society for Psychical Research in 1882. Its founder members included many remarkable men like the poet Tennyson, Prime Minister Gladstone, the scientist J. J.

Thomson (discoverer of the electron), Mark Twain, Willian James, Lewis Carroll, John Ruskin, and Sir Oliver Lodge. Many of them had had their own curious experiences of the supernatural. For example, Ruskin (the famous art critic), spent a great deal of his time in Switzerland and heard about a place in the valley of Chamounix that was haunted by the ghost of a woman who raked dead leaves, and when she looked up her face was only a skull. But apparently this ghost could only be seen by children. So Ruskin sent to a neighboring valley for a child who knew nothing about the legend, and took him along to the spot which had been pointed out to him as haunted. Once there, he said to the boy, "What a lonely place! There's nobody here but ourselves!" "Yes there is," said the child, "there's a woman over there raking the leaves." "Let's go nearer to her," said Ruskin and let the boy lead the way. Suddenly, the boy stopped and said he did not want to go any further for the woman had looked up, and he said that she had no eyes in her head, "only holes."

A Lost Love

Arthur Balfour may have been interested in the question of life after death for a deeply personal reason. He had been in love with a girl called Mary Catherine Lyttelton, but had never asked her to marry him. He was nevertheless fairly sure that she would. Unfortunately, she died on Palm Sunday, 1875. Balfour remained unmarried for the rest of his life – it is believed

*The woman on the left was claimed to have psychic powers,
seen here with her daughter, son and another, 1930s.
(Courtesy of Alastair Maclean).*

– because he was faithful to the memory of Mary Lyttelton. But Balfour himself apparently also had certain psychic powers. The well-known author Andrew Lang, who also wrote about ghosts, tells how he lent a crystal ball to Balfour's sister and her brother happened to see it, laughed at her and took it into his study. Not long afterwards, he came out looking very puzzled. He had been looking into the crystal when suddenly he saw a woman he knew sitting under a table lamp. He told his sister that he would find out the following Tuesday whether his vision had been correct. That Tuesday, Balfour went to a dance in Edinburgh and met the lady he had seen – her name was Miss Grant. Balfour said to her, "On Sunday at 5p.m., you were seated under a standard lamp, making tea. A man in a blue serge suit was beside you, with his back towards me. I saw the tip of his moustache. You wore a dress . . . ." (and Balfour then went on to describe it) ". . . . that I have never seen you wearing." The astonished lady admitted that he was right in every detail, and they both wrote out a report of the incident and signed it.

Soon after this incident, Balfour went along to have lunch with Andrew Lang. They talked about an investigator called Ada Goodrich-Freer. After lunch, sitting in Lang's study, Balfour was smoking and gazing into a glass bowl of water (presumably a fish bowl.) Suddenly he saw in it a room in a house, noticing the flooring, doors, windows and the staircase. A white Persian cat came walking down the stairs. The picture lasted quite a long time and Lang drew down the blinds while Balfour described it in detail. Later, Lang happened to meet Ada Goodrich-Freer, whom Balfour had never met and described what Balfour had seen in the glass bowl. "That is my house and my Persian cat!" said the lady. Lang had never been inside Ada Goodrich-Freer's house, but later on he visited it and saw that Balfour's description was absolutely accurate. So Balfour was another with good reason to be interested in psychical research.

A few years later, he had an even more personal reason – seemingly a series of messages from the girl he loved, Mary Lyttelton. It came about in rather a strange way. Myers, one of the most influential members of the Society, died in 1901. He had promised his friend Oliver Lodge that he would try to "return," and had given Lodge a message in a sealed envelope. He asked Lodge not to open this unless some "medium" came along to him with a message which purported to come from Myers. After Myers's death, one of his friends, Margaret Verrall, decided to try and contact him through automatic writing. After a while, a message came through in rather poor Latin signed "Myers." And soon after that another statement, "Myers's sealed envelope left with Lodge . . . . it has in it the words from the *Symposium* about love bridging the chasm."

The Verralls lost no time passing this on to Lodge, who opened the envelope. At first, it seemed that Myers was completely wrong. The message in the envelope said, "If I can revisit any earthly scene, I should choose the valley in the grounds of Hallsteads, Cumberland." That certainly did not seem to have anything to do with Plato and the *Symposium*, his famous dialogue on love. Then suddenly somebody remembered that Myers *had* referred to the *Symposium* in a privately-printed book called *Fragments of an Inner Life*. The book had been written as a memorial to Annie Marshall, the wife of Myers's cousin Walter, with whom Myers had been in love. Annie had committed suicide by drowning herself in Ullswater, and had lived in Hallsteads, Cumberland. It looked as if the spirit of Myers had made a slight mistake and imagined that his note about the place where Annie had lived, had actually contained the reference to Plato's *Symposium*.

What then happened is one of the most famous stories of psychical research – also one of the most complicated. In his book *Human Personality*, Myers had remarked that if the "spirits" really wanted to prove their existence, the most convincing way would be to distribute a message between *several* "mediums," like pieces of a jigsaw puzzle. And this is what now began to happen. Several mediums began to receive messages signed "Myers," all of which confirmed one another. After a while, other "spirits" began to join in. These included Edmund Gurney, Henry Sidgwick (whose wife was Arthur Balfour's sister), Annie Marshall and Mary Lyttelton, the girl whose death had been so traumatic for Balfour.

A number of "mediums" also became involved. The first was Rudyard Kipling's sister, Alice Flemying, who lived in India. Trying automatic writing one day, she received a message from Myers which told her to contact Margaret Verrall, and gave Mrs Verrall's

The Right Hon. A. J. Balfour, MP

correct address of 5 Selwyn Gardens, Cambridge. Another two "mediums" who became drawn into this complicated game were Mrs Leonora Piper and Mrs Winifred Coombe-Tennant.

Now Mary Lyttelton had died on Palm Sunday, 1875. Balfour had recently told her that he loved her and intended to propose next time he saw her. Unfortunately, she caught the typhoid bug and died. Balfour had spent every Palm Sunday since then – no matter how busy he was – with Mary's sister Lavinia, thinking and talking about her. Being an extremely secretive man, he told no one else about this. He also kept secret the fact that Mary had been buried wearing an emerald ring which had belonged to Balfour's mother. And only he and Lavinia shared another secret – that during Mary's last illness, her beautiful hair had been cut off and Balfour had later had a decorated silver box made to hold it. He also had a treasured photograph of Mary, in which she was wearing a three-stranded pearl necklace and carrying a lighted candle.

When the various mediums began to receive messages about Palm Sunday, and about a girl who was referred to as the "Palm Maiden" they were puzzled at this latest piece of the jigsaw puzzle. They were also puzzled at references to an emerald ring, long hair kept in a silver box and the photograph of the pearl necklace and candle. It was only gradually that they began to put the pieces of the jigsaw together and realize that the messages concerned Arthur Balfour and his lost love. One message referred to "King Arthur," and quoted Tennyson's *Ode on the Death of the Duke of Wellington*, who happened to be Arthur Balfour's godfather. It was clues like this that finally led Balfour's sister, Eleanor Sidgwick, to go to her brother and tell him that they seemed to be receiving messages that were intended for him. Eleanor Sidgwick has never revealed what happened at that meeting, except that her brother was "intensely interested" and that he remarked, "But all that happened nearly 40 years ago."

In 1916, Arthur Balfour went and sat with Mrs Coombe-Tennant while she produced automatic writing. The script she produced was signed "M," and referred to the writer as "the May Flower" (Mary had died in May), and described "a slender girl with hair worn in heavy plaits." Mrs Coombe-Tennent was trying to describe what she saw. "I see her standing in the glade of a park – over-arching trees." Balfour murmured, "I understand." Mrs Coombe-Tennent even described Balfour as he had been 40 years before, "A young man with rather curly hair parted in the middle and small semi-whiskers." When Balfour asked whether this was his brother, the "medium" replied that this young man seemed to be associated with the sword Excalibur – King Arthur. A reference to hair cut from a woman's head left Balfour in no doubt that it was Mary who was trying to communicate with him.

When Balfour was on his death-bed in March 1930, his sister Eleanor was in the room with him and also his sister-in-law, Lady Jean Balfour. They were playing records of Handel's *Messiah* and Lady Jean suddenly had an overpowering impression that the room was full of light and that there were unseen presences clustered around Balfour's bed. Balfour himself looked totally peaceful and contented. Suddenly his face changed and he was shaken with a stroke. But to Lady Jean's astonishment, the feeling of light and peace still filled the room and she felt that the unseen presences had actually wanted it to happen. She wrote later that it had been "merely a fierce effort to cast off the body and set free a soul." Balfour died peacefully a few days later.

Bettiscombe House, Dorset, ranks with Borley Rectory as one of the most famous haunted houses in England. The Queen Anne house, overlooking Marshwood Vale, is haunted by a screaming skull. In 1685, John and Azariah Pinney, the sons of the Revd John Pinney, took part in the unsuccessful Monmouth Rebellion and were both sentenced to death by Judge Jeffreys. John was executed but Azariah was sent to the West Indies as a slave.

When he finally returned to England, he was accompanied by a negro servant, who was in fact a slave. But the negro hated being in England, particularly in rural Dorset, where the natives thought that a man with a black skin was a kind of devil. He also reacted badly to the foggy weather of Marshwood Vale and eventually died of a chest ailment. His last request was that he should be buried in his home in Nevis in the West Indies.

This was impossible unless Azariah Pinney made the extremely long journey back there, with the consequence that he was buried in the old church yard of Bettiscombe.

There are conflicting accounts about how the skull came to be kept in the house. According to Guy Playfair, screams resounded through the house until finally the body was exhumed and sent back to the West Indies. Another account says that the screams resounded from the grave itself and that the body was removed and reburied elsewhere. For some reason, the skull was separated from the body and ended in Bettiscombe House.

From that time on, the skull has been kept there – in a room at the top of the house. In the course of the years, the jaw has disappeared and only the upper half of the skull remains. Whenever there has been an attempt to remove it from the house and bury it, the screaming sounds have become so terrifying that it has been hastily returned. The present owners (descendants of the original Pinneys), believe that if the skull is taken from the house, the owner will die within the year. That may be why they have refused several requests from ghost-hunters to bury the skull again and test whether this results in a resumption of the screaming sounds.

Apparitions

The Society for Psychical Research soon became a flourishing organisation. And one of its first major publications was a vast work in two volumes, more than 1,400 pages long, called *Phantasms of the Living*. The title is rather misleading because it contains just as many cases of ghosts, or apparitions of the dead. No one would want to read *Phantasms of the Living* from beginning to end because it would soon become monotonous. Case after case is about someone who has a sudden flash of knowledge that someone they knew is dead. The following is typical: "I was going from the house I lived at to a shop kept by my brother, and when about half-way, it came on to rain very fast. I called in at the house of a lady friend and waited some time, but it did not clear and, as I was afraid my brother would be leaving, I said I must go. I rose to do so and went into the hall, and my friend rushed away upstairs to get an umbrella, leaving me in the dark. In the higher part of the door was a glass window, and all at once, in the darkness, I saw a face looking through that window. The face was very well known to me, though for the instant I did not associate it with the original, as she was 300 miles away. I instantly opened the door and found nobody there, and then searched the ivy with which the porch and house are covered. Finding nothing, and knowing that it was impossible anyone could have got away, I then for the first time inquired of myself whose was the face I had seen. I at once knew that the face was that of a married sister-in-law of my wife's. I told all our family of the circumstances directly I got home, and judge of our dismay when we had a letter to say that she had died at the very hour I saw her. Monday was the evening I saw her face, and on Wednesday, when we were at dinner, the letter came. It is signed T. W. Goodyear. Various members of his family also write letters confirming that this is exactly what happened."

Here is another from the Revd R. Markham-Hill: "On the evening of Easter Sunday, about eight or nine years ago, I think, I was just beginning my supper, feeling very tired after the day's work, when I saw the door opening behind me. I was sitting with my back to the door, but could just see it over my shoulder. I may also have heard the opening, but cannot speak with certainty on this point. I turned half round, and just had time to see the figure of a tall man rushing hastily into the room, as if to attack me. I sprang up at once, turned round, and threw the glass I held in my hand, at the spot where I had seen the figure, which had disappeared in the act of my rising. The disappearance had, however, been too sudden to arrest the act of throwing. I then realized that I had seen an apparition, and I immediately connected it with one of my uncles whom I knew to be seriously ill. Moreover, the figure which I saw resembled my uncle in stature. Mr Adcock came in, and found me quite unnerved by the occurrence and to him I related the circumstances. I don't remember telling him that I connected the vision with my uncle. The next day a telegram came announcing my uncle's death on the Sunday. My father was summoned to my uncle's death-bed unexpectedly on the Sunday evening as he was sitting at supper, and the death must have coincided in time with what I saw."

Doppelgängers

But not all the cases are as straightforward as this. One of the accounts is by a woman called Sarah Hall, who describes how, in the autumn of 1863, she was living with her husband and baby in a house which had once been a church, near Northampton. Her married cousin and her husband were visiting. One night, as they were sitting eating supper, a "ghost" appeared by the sideboard. The odd thing was that the ghost was Sarah Hall herself. Her husband saw it first and exclaimed, "It is Sarah!" And then they all four looked across the room, to see a woman who looked exactly like Sarah Hall standing there in a spotted summer dress – not one that Sarah Hall recognized. A moment later, the "ghost" disappeared. Sarah Hall comments that she was not in the least worried or afraid – it was rather like looking at a picture or a statue. In other words, the "ghost" did not appear to be alive. The odd thing is that two years later, Mrs Hall *did* possess a spotted summer dress like the one she had seen on her "ghost." The only clue that makes any sense is Mrs Hall's comment that the house used to be a church. Christian churches were frequently built on old pagan sites, as if the ground had some kind of inherent "power" or force. Obviously, what Mrs Hall had seen was simply her own "doppelgänger," or double.

The poet, Goethe, has described in his autobiography how he once saw his own doppelgänger. He was 22 at the time, and had just said farewell to a girl he was in love with. He writes, "I now rode on horseback over the footpath to Drusenheim, when one of the strangest experiences befell me. Not with the eyes of the body, but with those of the spirit, I saw myself on horseback coming towards me on the same path dressed in a suit such as I had never worn, pale-gray with some gold. As soon as I had shaken myself out of this reverie, the form vanished. It is strange, however, that I found myself returning on the same path eight years afterwards, to visit Frederika once more, and that I then wore the suit I had dreamt of, and that this was not by design, but by chance.

"Be this as it may, the strange phantasm had a calming influence on my feelings in those moments following the parting."

In fact, it is almost as if Goethe's unconscious mind was able to foresee the future and was able to comfort him by telling him that he would be returning later to see Frederika.

Now several members of Goethe's family had "psychic powers," including his mother, his sister and his grandfather. His grandfather often dreamed of the future. Goethe tells how his grandfather had dreamed that he was at a council meeting – where he was a junior alderman – when suddenly one of the senior councillors had arisen from his seat, walked down the steps to Goethe's grandfather and indicated his own chair in a most gracious manner suggesting that he should take the seat. Then the councillor walked out of the room. Goethe's grandfather told his wife that he would become a councillor when the next vacancy occurred. In fact, the councillor who had offered him his seat died shortly afterwards of a stroke and his position was offered to Goethe's grandfather.

He had a similar glimpse of the future one day when he was awakened at midnight by a messenger, who summoned all the councillors to a midnight meeting. The mayor had just died and the councillors had to draw lots about who was going to be the next mayor –

they were in such a hurry in case the Emperor exercised his prerogative of appointing the next mayor. The messenger asked if he could have a candle stump because his candle had almost gone out. "Give him a whole one," said Goethe's grandfather, "he has had all this trouble on account of me." And in fact, when the councillors drew lots to see who would be mayor, it was Goethe's grandfather.

A Glimpse of the Future

Now stories like these sound like a contradiction of the laws of time. It should be impossible to foresee the future because the future has not happened. "Spirits" seem to experience no such problem. If we recall the case recounted by Heirich Werner in the last chapter, in which a father went and pulled his daughter back into a room when she was about to fall out of the window, we can see that this involved foreseeing the future. The father felt uneasy while he was sitting in his office, went home and went upstairs, just in time to grab his daughter's dress as she leaned out of the window. Obviously, she was not already hanging out of the window when he felt uneasy in his office. Werner's psychic patient R.O. claimed that it was Albert, her guardian spirit, who warned her father. How did Albert know that the little girl was going to lean out of the window?

The same question arises in an interesting case in *Phantasms of the Living*. An American surgeon named Ormsby describes how, during the American Civil

War, he had realized that a young sergeant named Albert Adams was seriously ill and was likely to die. He had him removed from the military hospital to a private house and telegraphed for the sergeant's father to come. At 11.00 p.m., Albert Adams apparently died. Ormsby led the father to a chair, afraid that he was about to faint. But when he came back, the dead man was lying there with his eyes wide open and asked in a normal tone of voice: "Doctor, what day of the month is it?" When the doctor told him he answered, "That is the day I died." Then he looked at his father, who was now standing by the bedside and said, "Father, our boys have taken Fort Henry, and Charlie [his brother] isn't hurt. I've seen mother and the children, and they are well." He then talked for about five minutes about his own funeral, giving full instructions. After that he asked again; "Doctor, what day of the month is it," and when the doctor told him once again. He repeated, "That's the day I died," and immediately died. He later proved correct – Fort Henry had been taken and his brother Charlie had not been hurt. He seems to have seen his own death *as if it was in the past*, together with the date.

We might, of course, assume that the phrase, "That was the day I died," was simply a dying man speaking in a kind of fever. But we have to recollect that he was speaking in a normal, clear voice and that he had just seen that Fort Henry had been taken and that his brother was safe.

It begins to look as if our material world, which looks so solid and reliable, may be some sort of illusion – or at least, something far more strange and complex than we imagine. To begin with, if Sarah Hall could see her own ghost, it begins to look as if the ghost existed as much in her mind as in the world of reality. Or perhaps it existed in some strange intermediate world midway between the mind and objective reality.

We began this book by talking about how Colonel Meadows-Taylor saw a "ghost" of the girl he loved, and who was about to be married. It seems clear that he saw it because she was thinking about him at the time, and her thought somehow reached across the thousands of miles between them and somehow made her appear physically solid.

Then, what about Lord Henry Brougham's vision of his schoolfriend G., sitting on the chair beside his bath? Is it not possible that G. was also thinking about him, and that G.'s thought somehow made Lord Brougham see him?

It begins to look as if this question of life after death is rather more complicated than it first appears.

5

Ghost Detectives

In his autobiography *Celebrities and Simple Souls*
(1933), the playwright Alfred Sutro has an interesting
ghost story. He explains that it is the only psychic
experience he has ever had in his whole life.

He tells of being driven along a country road by his
chauffeur when he thought he heard the wail of a
child. He asked the chauffeur to stop. The man said he
could hear nothing, but Sutro followed the sound
behind some trees and down the slope of a river
bank. There he found a pretty child of three or four,
crying and sobbing. She was soaking wet and had
obviously fallen into the water. He carried her back
to the car, but was unable to make her stop crying long
enough to tell him what had happened. He asked her
where she lived and pointed down the road ahead. The
little girl nodded so the chauffeur drove on. Not far
away they came to a gate and the child pointed
towards it. They drove along a drive to the front door
of a "largish house," and as the car pulled up a man
and a woman rushed out to meet it. "Have you any
news of the child?" "She's back there in the car," said
Sutro and took them back to it. But the car was empty.

"Where's the little girl?" he asked the chauffeur, but the man looked blank. "The child I brought to the car." "You didn't bring any child to the car," he replied. They drove back to the river bank; the body of the child was lying in a few feet of water . . . .

An extraordinary story, certainly, but one which most people would dismiss as preposterous. However, there is a certain amount of circumstantial evidence in its favour. Sutro was a famous playwright in the Edwardian era and would presumably not tell lies for the fun of it. And the fact that it was his only psychic experience, also suggests that it was genuine.

It was not. Sutro states that he has told the story to various people who dabble in the psychic and occult and that he has been offered various explanations. But he has never been offered the true one, which is that he made it up. It was evidently intended to demonstrate the gullibility of people who believe in ghosts . . . .

Once we know that, we can begin to see the weaknesses in the story. Would a man driving in a car hear the crying of a child? And even if he did, would he bother to stop to investigate? – crying children are not all that rare. Would the chauffeur not have asked him what on earth he was doing as he talked to an empty seat next to him and asked where it lived? Would he have got out of the car at the front door, leaving the child behind in the car? These are the kind of questions we have to ask about a "supernatural" experience if we wish to avoid being taken in. This is why the Society for Psychical Research took so much trouble to get witnesses to sign sworn statements.

Most ghost stories of the past have something absurd about them. Even if they were originally true, they have been touched up in the telling.

The Red Barn Murder

One of the favorite themes of old ghost stories is murderers who have been haunted by the ghost of the victim, sometimes rattling chains and giving horrible screams, until the murderer goes mad or feels obliged to hand himself over to the law.

Real ghosts do not behave like this. But there are, nevertheless, a number of such tales that bear the stamp of authenticity. One of the most famous was the Red Barn murder, which was turned into one of the most popular plays of the nineteenth century.

In May 1827, a farmer's son named William Corder lured his pregnant mistress Maria Marten, into a barn in Polstead, Suffolk, where he shot her. Maria was buried in a corner of the barn and Corder soon afterwards left for London, where he married and became a schoolmaster. But Maria's stepmother, who was known for her "second sight," began to have nightmares in which she was in the red barn and saw the ground open up, to reveal Maria's corpse. She was even able to state the precise spot – underneath the right hand bay on the further side of the barn. The barn did not belong to Maria's father – who was an ordinary farm worker – but he eventually managed to get into the barn with the excuse of looking for some clothes his daughter might have left there. He went to the right hand bay, moved some corn and found some huge stones lying there. The handle of a rake showed that the earth was soft and yielding. Marten and a farm bailiff removed a few inches of earth and found an iron spike. A few feet further down was the body of Maria Marten, tied up in a sack. Corder was arrested in London, and in April 1828, was publicly hanged in front of the Bury St Edmunds jail.

Of course, we do not have to assume – as the Victorians did – that it was Maria Marten's spirit that made her stepmother dream about the place where she was buried. Corder had asked her to go to the barn dressed in men's clothes so that she would not be recognized if anyone saw her. (He told her they were about to elope.) She seems to have been in the process of changing out of her men's clothes when Corder murdered her, so it is probable that she was in the bay where her body was later found – it is natural for anyone getting undressed to look for some place of concealment, as well as somewhere they can hang the clothes that they remove. Corder seems to have shot her then used a knife – or the iron spike – to stab her. It follows that her death was not instantaneous. Anne Marten could have received the telepathic message about the place of the murder as Maria was dying – but it remained unconscious until it presented itself to her as a recurrent dream.

Eric Tombe and Ernest Dyer

But there are other cases where this kind of explanation fails to cover the facts. In April 1922, a young ex-army officer named Eric Tombe disappeared. He had been in business with a man named Ernest Dyer, running a racing stable at Kenley in Surrey. The stable had not been very successful but when it burned down, an insurance investigator found empty petrol cans in the ruins and Dyer dropped the claim. He had been borrowing money from Eric Tombe and the two men quarrelled. Then Tombe vanished and Dyer went off to the North of England (where he used various aliases, and passed dud cheques.) In November 1922, when police came to question him about suspected fraud he pulled a revolver from his pocket and, in the ensuing struggle, accidentally shot himself. In his room, police found Eric Tombe's cheque book (with forged signatures), and Tombe's passport with Dyer's photograph substituted.

Eric Tombe's father, the Revd Gordon Tombe, was the vicar of a village in Oxfordshire – Little Tew. In April 1922, Mrs Tombe began to dream that her son was dead and that he was lying buried down a well, with a stone slab over its mouth. It seemed to be in the grounds of a farm. The vicar gave up his living and moved to Sydenham, in order to devote himself to finding his son. He called at Eric's Haymarket flat and from neighbors learned about the stud farm – "The Welcomes" – at Kenley. The farm proved to be in ruins but Ernest Dyer's wife was still living there. She told Tombe that her husband was dead – that he had been killed in a road crash that summer. She had no idea what had become of Eric. The vicar went to Scotland Yard – the police discovered that many cheques had been drawn on Eric Tombe's bank account since his disappearance in April.

Finally, to humor Mrs Tombe – who continued to dream that her son was down a well – the police searched "The Welcomes." There was no well, but on the edge of the paddock there were four cess-pits, each covered with a heavy slab. The first three were empty but the fourth was full of rubble. This was removed and revealed an arched recess. In this was the corpse of Eric Tombe. He had been shot in the back of the head with a shotgun. At the inquest, the jury returned a verdict of murder by Ernest Dyer. It was only after the death of "Mr Fitzsimmons" in Scarborough, two months later, that the police realized they had located Ernest Dyer.

Since Tombe had been shot in the back of the head – which blasted away his skull – he must have died instantly. In that case, it would have been impossible for him to have transmitted to his mother a telepathic message about being buried down a "well." (Mrs Tombe, of course, saw the cess-pit in her dreams and assumed that it was a well.) The only other person from whose mind Mrs Tombe might have picked up this information was Dyer himself, and since Mrs Tombe did not know of his existence, this seems unlikely. It is difficult to resist the inference that Eric Tombe somehow communicated with his mother after death.

Mona Tinsley

In one of the most celebrated murder cases of the 1930s, a dead child described what had happened to her and led to the conviction of her killer.

On January 5, 1937, a ten-year-old girl named Mona Tinsley failed to return home from her school in Newark, Nottinghamshire. A neighbor of the Tinsley family reported seeing the ex-lodger, a man called Frederick Nodder, loitering near the school. Two other people said that they had seen Mona with a middle-aged man near the bus station. Nodder, who was living in the village of Hayton, some 20 miles from Newark, denied all knowledge of the child but was taken into custody on a bastardy warrant. Nodder had, in fact, been introduced to the Tinsleys by Mrs Tinsley's sister, with whom he was having an affair. A few days after his arrest, Nodder changed his story and admitted that he had met Mona in Newark and taken her home with him. But he insisted that he had put her on a bus to Sheffield, where his mistress lived. Nodder was charged with abducting Mona Tinsley (in the absence of a body he could not be charged with murder), and sentenced to seven years in jail.

A few days after Mona's disappearance, Estelle Roberts, one of the most celebrated "mediums" in England at the time, offered to help the police. Mona's parents agreed and the police sent her a pink silk dress that had belonged to Mona. In her autobiography, *Fifty Years a Medium*, Estelle Roberts writes, "As . . . . I held the soft material in my hands, I knew that Mona was dead." The "medium" then – according to her own account – addressed Mona Tinsley directly, through the agency of her "control," a red Indian called Red Cloud. The child told her that she had been

Estelle Roberts goes into a trance

taken to a house and strangled and Estelle Roberts "saw" a small house, with a water-filled ditch on one side, a field behind, a graveyard nearby and an inn not far away. She seemed to travel across fields to the river.

When she described the house to the Newark police, they were so impressed by her accuracy that they invited her to go there and sent a police car to fetch her from the railway station. The house looked exactly as she had "seen" it. She was allowed to wander around inside, and in the back bedroom sensed the child's presence, particularly near a water tank. She was able to tell the police that Mona had slept in the back bedroom, and learned that they had found a child's handkerchief in the water tank. Mona was strangled in the back bedroom. She had spent much of her time in the downstairs front room, copying something out of a book. The police had found scraps of paper with child's writing on it. The medium added that, after killing her, Nodder had left the house with the body by the side door. The police asked, "Why not the front door?" and she admitted she had no idea. They told her that the front door had been permanently closed with screws. She then led the police past the graveyard she had "seen," over a bridge and across the fields. She told them, "Beyond these fields there is a river. You will find the child's body there."

The police had already dragged the river without success. But they now had good reason for supposing that the body would be found in the river. In her introduction to *The Trial of Frederick Nodder*, Winifred Duke states, "A clairvoyant insisted that Mona Tinsley was dead and had appeared to her. The child declared

113

that she had been strangled, her body placed in a sack, and then conveyed on wheels to the water and thrown in." Another "medium" told Mr Tinsley that Mona would be found in the river Idle. The "medium" had tasted mud in her mouth. A third woman informed the Newark police that Mona's body would be recovered in water, at a place 30 miles in a north-westerly direction from Newark, "close to an open meadow or pasture land, with tall trees lining the bank."

In June 1937, a boating party on the river Idle noticed an object in the water close to the bank – it proved to be Mona Tinsley's body, the head jammed in a drain below the water level. The place corresponded closely to the "medium's" description. A sack with an odor of decaying flesh was found nearby. Nodder was tried a second time and although he still strenuously denied killing Mona, he was sentenced to death.

Teresita Basa

One of the most remarkable and well-authenticated cases of a murder victim returning from the dead, led to some violent legal arguments about whether a ghost can be regarded as a reliable witness. It was the case of a Filipino physical therapist named Teresita Basa, who was stabbed to death in Chicago on February 21, 1977. Toward 8.30 p.m. of that day, the Chicago fire department was called to put out a blaze in a high-rise apartment building on the North Side.

Two firefighters crawled into Apartment 15B, through black smoke, and saw that the fire was in the bedroom. A mattress lying at the foot of the bed was blazing. Within minutes the firemen had put the blaze out and opened the windows to let out the smoke. When they lifted the waterlogged mattress they found the naked body of a woman, with her legs spread apart and a knife sticking out of her chest. 48-year-old Teresita Basa had been born in the city of Damaguete, in the Philippines, the daughter of a judge. She had become a physical therapist specializ ing in respiratory problems – perhaps because her father had died of a respiratory illness – and was working at Edgewater Hospital in Chicago at the time of her death.

Forensic examination postulated that Teresita had answered the door to someone she knew – she had been talking to a friend on the telephone when the doorbell rang. The intruder had encircled her neck from behind with his arm and choked her until she lost consciousness. He had then taken money from her handbag and ransacked the apartment. After that he had stripped off all her clothes, taken a butcher knife from the kitchen drawer and driven it virtually through her body. Then he had set the mattress on fire with a piece of burning paper, dumped it on top of her and hurried out of the apartment. The fire alarm had sounded before he had gone more than a few blocks. Forensic investigation also revealed that there had been no sexual assault. Teresita Basa had died a virgin.

Although Remy (short for Remibias) Chua, another Filipino, had worked with Teresita Basa in the respiratory therapy department of Edgewater Hospital, the two had been only slightly acquainted. Two weeks after the murder, during the course of a conversation, Mrs Chua remarked (only half seriously), "If there is no solution to her murder, she can come to me in a dream." She then went for a brief nap in the hospital locker room – it was 2.00 a.m. As she was dozing on a chair, her feet propped on another, something made her open her eyes. She had to suppress a scream as she saw Teresita Basa – looking as solid as a living person – standing in front of her. She lost no time in running out of the room.

During the course of the next few weeks, two of Mrs Chua's fellow employees jokingly remarked that she looked – and behaved – like Teresita Basa. Her husband, Dr Jose Chua, also noticed that his wife seemed to have undergone a personality change. Normally sunny and good-natured, she had become oddly peremptory and moody. Teresita Basa had also been prone to moods.

In late July, five months after the murder, Remy Chua was working with a hospital orderly named Allan Showery when she found herself experiencing an inexplicable panic. Showery was a sinewy but powerfully built black man with an open and confident manner. When Showery was standing behind Mrs Chua, she caught a movement out of the corner of her eye – just as Teresita may have when her killer stepped up behind her to lock his forearm round her neck – and, inexplicably, her heart began to pound violently. She decided she was suffering from nervous problems and asked for time off work. That night her husband heard her talking in her sleep – she was repeating, "Al – Al – Al . . . ." She told him later that she had dreamed of being in a smoke-filled room. The next day she felt so ill that she asked her parents to come over. After taking a strong sedative, she climbed into bed. But after a few hours' sleep she began to babble in Spanish – a language Remy Chua did not speak. Her husband knelt beside the bed and asked, "How are you?" His wife replied, "I am Teresita Basa." When Jose Chua asked what she wanted, the voice replied, "I want help. . . . nothing has been done about the man who killed me." A few minutes later "Teresita" disappeared and Remy Chua was herself again.

Two days later, Remy Chua felt a pain in her chest followed by a heavy sensation, "as if someone was stepping into her body." She told her mother (who was still with them), "Terrie is here again." When her husband returned he found his wife in bed. The voice of Teresita Basa issued from her mouth, asking accusingly, "Did you talk to the police?" Jose Chua acknowledged that he had not because he needed proof. "Allan killed me," insisted the voice. "I let Al into the apartment and he killed me."

The strain of Remy Chua's "possession" was beginning to adversely affect the whole family (the Chuas had four children). Jose Chua finally went to his boss at Franklin Park Hospital, Dr Winograd, and told him the whole story. Dr Winograd took the "possession" seriously but believed that the police would dismiss it as an absurdity. He advised Dr Chua to write them an anonymous letter.

The "possessing entity" had other ideas. The next

time Remy Chua went into a trancelike state, the voice demanded to know why Jose Chua had not done as she asked. He explained that he had no proof. "Dr Chua," said the voice, "the man Allan Showery stole my jewellery and gave it to his girlfriend. They live together."

"But how could it be identified?"

"My cousins, Ron Somera and Ken Basa, could identify it. So could my friends, Richard Pessoti and Ray King." She went on to give Ron Somera's telephone number to Dr Chua. After that she told him, "Al came to fix my television and he killed me and burned me. Tell the police."

Dr Chua finally decided to do as she asked – he telephoned the Evanston police headquarters. On August 8, 1977, Investigator Joseph Stachula was assigned to interview the Chuas. Their story left him stunned, yet he had an intuitive certainty that they were not cranks. All the same, he could see no obvious way to make use of what they had told him. He could hardly walk up to Allan Showery and arrest him on the grounds that his victim had come back from the dead to accuse him. A check on Showery revealed that he might well be the killer. He had a long criminal record that included two rapes, each of which had taken place in the victim's apartment. Moreover, he had lived only four blocks from Teresita Basa.

Showery was brought to the police station and was asked if it were true that he had agreed to repair Teresita Basa's television on the evening of her murder. He acknowledged that it was, but insisted that he had gone to a local bar for a drink and simply forgotten. Asked if he had ever been in the Basa apartment, he denied it. Then, when asked for finger-print samples to compare with some found in the apartment, he changed his mind and acknowledged that he had been there some months earlier. Finally, he admitted that he had been there on the evening of her death but claimed that he had left immediately because he did not have a circuit plan for that particular television.

Now the suspect was obviously nervous and the interviewers left him alone while they went back to talk to Yanka, Showery's girlfriend. She recalled that on the evening of the murder – she remembered it because the fire engine had passed her window – Showery had come home early. Asked by the inter-viewers if he had recently given her any jewellery, she showed them an antique cocktail ring. She was asked to accompany them back to the police station, to-gether with her jewellery box. Meanwhile, Teresita Basa's two friends, Richard Pessoti and Ray King, were brought to the station. As soon as Pessoti glimpsed the ring on Yanka's finger, he recognized it as one belong-ing to Teresita Basa. The two were also able to identify other jewellery in Yanka's jewellery box.

Stachula's partner, Detective Lee Epplen, con-fronted Showery and told him, "It's all over." Show-ery screamed angrily, "You cops are trying to frame me." When shown the jewellery, he insisted that he had bought it at a pawn shop but had failed to get a receipt. Minutes later he realized that the evidence against him was overwhelming. He asked to speak to Yanka and in the presence of the detectives said,

"Yanka, I have something to tell you. I killed Teresita Basa."

He had believed that Teresita was rich and that robbing her would solve all his financial problems. But after killing her, he found that her purse contained only $30. In order to make the murder look like a sex crime, he had undressed her and spread her legs apart. Then he had stabbed her with the butcher knife and set the mattress on fire, hoping that the fire would destroy any clues he might have left behind.

The "Voice from the Grave" case made national headlines. Showery came to trial on January 21, 1979, before Judge Frank W. Barbero. But the story of the "possession" of Remy Chua was so astounding that the jury was unable to agree on a verdict. The defense also objected that the evidence of a ghost was not admissible in a court of law. Five days later, a mistrial was declared. But on February 23, 1979, Allan Showery acknowledged that he was guilty of the murder of Teresita Basa. He was sentenced to 14 years for murder and to four years each on charges of armed robbery and arson.

Psychic Detectives

In the twentieth century, there have been many notable "psychic detectives," like Peter Hurkos and Gerard Croiset, but they usually claim to have solved their cases by "psychometry." This means the ability to "read" the history of an object by holding it in the hands. A history of psychometry would occupy more space than we have available, but one example will show its accuracy. In the winter of 1921, a number of people had come together in a room of the Metapsychic Institute – the French version of the Society for Psychical Research – in Paris, to test a clairvoyant, Mme de B. Dr Gustav Geley, a leading French investigator and director of the Institute, asked someone to pass a letter to her. A painter and novelist called Pascal Forthuny grabbed it. "It can't be difficult to invent something that applies to anybody!" He began to improvise jokingly, "Ah yes, I sec a crime . . . . a murder . . . ." When he had finished, Dr Geley said, "That letter was from Henri Landru." Landru was at that time on trial for the murder of 11 women – crimes for which he was guillotined in the following year. No one was very impressed by Forthuny's performance. After all, Landru's trial was the chief news event of the day, so murder was an obvious topic to come into Forthuny's mind. Geley's wife picked up a fan from the table. "Let's see if that was just luck. Try this."

Still light-hearted, Forthuny ran his fingers over the fan in a professional manner and looked solemnly into space. "I have the impression of being suffocated. And I hear a name being called – Elisa!" Mme Geley looked at him in stupefaction. The fan had belonged to an old lady who had died seven years earlier from congestion of the lungs and the companion of her last days had been called Elisa.

Now it was Forthuny's turn to suspect a joke. But Mme Geley insisted on another experiment. She handed him an officer's cane. This time Forthuny looked serious as he let his fingers stray over it. He spoke of the young French officer who had owned the cane, of his return to France by sea and of how the ship was torpedoed. He went on to say that the officer was rescued but had developed an illness and died two years later. Mme Geley verified that he was right in every detail.

For the novelist, it was one of the most bewildering moments of his life. He found himself thinking, "Do I possess a faculty I do not even suspect?" Mme Geley handed him a letter and Forthuny passed it between his hands before he said, "This letter was written in a beautiful city – the Orient. What a magnificent view and what a blue sky!" It had, in fact, been written in Constantinople by her father.

The skeptic Forthuny went on to become one of the most celebrated "psychometrists" of his time. Yet he also became a "medium" and found one day that his hand was doing automatic writing. This automatic writing came from his son Frederick, who had been killed in a plane crash in 1919. There was also a so-called "spirit guide", who proved to be irritable and touchy. He proposed to Forthuny that the two of them should collaborate on a book about "Art as a Servant of the Spirit." Forthuny agreed but as the work proceeded – his hand flying across the page at great speed – he began to find himself questioning some of the views of his guide and began to raise cautious objections. The guide promptly lost his temper and became vituperative – the hand wrote so fast that it became almost incoherent, rebuking him for his "maladroit imagination inspired by human vanity . . . ." Forthuny indignantly threw down his pen, but the next time he took it up received a blast of condemnation, "If you don't stop this arrogance I will abandon you. You just have the criminal thought of throwing the pen in my face. This would he your greatest sin since you were born . . . ." It becomes quite clear from all this that spirits can be just as vain and stupid as human beings.

Many psychometrists and "psychic detectives" are dubious about the existence of a spirit world. One of these is the modern psychic, Robert Cracknell, who has been instrumental in solving many criminal cases but who feels that the psychic faculty is something that all human beings possess, like the sense of sight or hearing. One of Cracknell's most remarkable successes occurred in 1977, when a pretty Australian girl named Janie Shepherd vanished on the streets of London. Janie left her flat in St Johns Wood on the evening of Friday, February 4, 1977, to spend the weekend with her boyfriend, Roddy Kinkead-Weekes, who lived in Knightsbridge. She was driving a red Mini, with a "For Sale" notice in the back window. She never reached Knightsbridge – both Janie and her car vanished.

Four days later, on February 8, the Mini was found in Elgin Crescent. It was streaked with mud and had several parking tickets under the windscreen wipers. By this time the police had been alerted and Chief Superintendent Henry Mooney, of Scotland Yard's Murder Squad, was called in. The interior of the car showed that a struggle had taken place and there were two knife slashes in the sun-roof. A petrol receipt in the car showed that Janie had topped up her tank not long before she vanished. From the amount of petrol that had been used, the police were able to deduce that the car had travelled about 75 miles.

Janie was the step-daughter of a wealthy Australian company executive and her parents immediately hurried to London to help in the search. Forensic examination of the mud revealed that it could have come from a number of places within 30 or so miles of London. Janie's parents spent days of driving around every one of them. But it would not be until Monday, April 18, that Janie's body was found by two school-boys in a wood on Nomansland Common, near Wheathampstead in Hertfordshire – within a hundred yards of where her parents had searched. Forensic examination revealed that she had been strangled and raped. Although she was fully clothed, she was – oddly enough – no longer wearing the clothes she had left home in. Her killer had taken the spare clothes she was carrying in a weekend bag and dressed her in them, even down to her underwear. Her original clothes had vanished. The killer was evidently afraid that the police might find some clue on them.

At the time the body was found, Bob Cracknell (who already had a considerable reputation as a psychic sleuth), was being interviewed by a freelance journalist. Cracknell had been a psychic ever since childhood, when he had had strange flashes of "vision" in which he saw actual scenes taking place. And one day, talking to a reporter who was investigating a £3 million swindle involving church organs, he had a vision of the swindlers in Ullapool in Scotland. That was where the police found them. And as a result of the case, Cracknell gained a reputation as a psychic who could help the police. The journalist finished the interview by asking casually, "You don't happen to have any impressions about the Janie Shepherd case?" As he spoke, Cracknell felt "as if someone had pressed the switch in my brain." He saw clearly a pretty blonde girl who had been violently attacked in the back of a red Mini – so violently that her contraceptive coil had been torn out and lay on the seat.

Intrigued by this detail, the reporter contacted Scotland Yard. That night he rang Cracknell. "No luck, Bob. No such device was found." Cracknell was startled and disappointed – it was the first time his "visions" had ever been wrong. But the next day he found a telegram from his friend. Detectives who knew the case better, knew that there *had* been a contraceptive device on the back seat. But this information had been kept secret. Hours later, two members of the Murder Squad were at Cracknell's door – his knowledge had made him a major suspect. Cracknell had to do some fast and convincing talking to establish that he was a psychic, not a killer. They asked him if he had any further impressions about Janie Shepherd. Suddenly he had another of his visions. He "saw" that the man who had killed Janie Shepherd had a scar on his cheek and was black. But he had yet another impression. "I think you've already got him for another rape." The police looked at one another and Cracknell suddenly knew he was correct. He was to write in his autobiography a few years later, "I am convinced that her killer is now serving a seven-year sentence for rape." The book, *Clues to the Unknown*, appeared in 1981. Cracknell was wrong in only one detail. Janie Shepherd's killer was serving a 12-year sentence for rape.

In 1864, a guard at the Tower of London was court-martialled for falling asleep on duty. He had been found lying on the ground, several yards from his sentry box, with his bayonet a few yards away.

The sentry, who belonged to the 60th Rifles, had a strange tale to tell. Standing guard in the mist, he had suddenly seen a figure walking towards him – it looked like a woman dressed in white. He shouted a challenge but the figure ignored him, so he charged with his bayonet. But the bayonet, he said, had gone straight through the woman, meeting no resistance, and he had fainted.

The sentry was lucky – his commander was able to support his story. Major General J. D. Dundas commanded the 60th Rifles quartered in the Tower of London. He had been looking out of a window in the Bloody Tower (where prisoners were kept before their execution), and had noticed the guard stationed at the door of the Lieutenant's Lodgings, outside the oak-beamed chamber where Queen Anne Boleyn, wife of Henry the VIII, spent her last days before her execution on June 19, 1536. He had actually seen the white figure walk out of the mist and had seen the sentry challenge her and then charge – and faint.

Dundas' evidence at the court-martial led to the acquittal of the sentry. So did the corroborative evidence of Field Marshal Lord Grenfell, who also said he had seen the white lady several times.

The Tower of London

In June 1976, a young woman had been parking her car late at night in Chesterton Street, Kensington, when a man asked her the time. He then pushed her into the car, drove to a railway arch and raped her at knife point. Finally, he slashed her wrist and ran away. She described him as a black man with a scarred cheek. When, a year later, the police were investigating Janie Shepherd's murder, they searched their files on sex offenders and came up with this unsolved case. They decided to interview all the men listed as suspects at the time. Among these was a man named David Lashley, born in St Lawrence, Barbados, where he had served one term for violent rape. But apparently the police had not interviewed Lashley at the time because his description did not mention a scarred cheek. Now Chief Superintendent Mooney repaired that omission – and found that Lashley *did* have a scar. He was identified by the young woman as her rapist and sent to prison for 12 years. There was, of course, no evidence to link him to Janie Shepherd – although the Murder Squad thought he was probably the killer.

Then they had a stroke of luck. In Frankland High Security Prison in Durham, Lashley used to spend hours in the gymnasium practising weightlifting. Another keep-fit fanatic was a rapist called Daniel Reece. One day, they were discussing a recent rape case when Lashley said, "He should have killed her. If I'd killed the one that landed me in here like I killed Janie Shepherd, I'd be a free man now." He went on to describe how he had abducted Janie Shepherd at knife point, driven to a dark spot in Ladbroke Grove and raped and strangled her. Then, with the corpse belted tightly with the seat belt, he had driven to Hertfordshire and disposed of the body.

At the time of the Janie Shepherd investigation, a young couple had reported how they had seen a red Mini being driven by a black man, with a blonde girl, apparently drunk, slewing around in the front seat. Reece repeated Lashley's story to a friendly prison officer, who finally persuaded him to talk to the police. As a result, Lashley was rearrested as he walked out of prison in April 1989.

At his trial in February 1990, Reece's detailed account of Lashley's confession was confirmed again and again by police records. Lashley's previous victims repeated their evidence concerning the violence of his earlier rapes and the hatred he expressed towards white women. Forensic examination of semen found in the Mini showed that it matched Lashley's. And when Mr Justice Alliott finally passed sentence, he made it clear that by "life imprisonment" he really meant life.

We have already noted the role of dreaming in psychic detection. The first person to bring this idea before a wide public was an aeronautical engineer and amateur physicist named J. W. Dunne. When Dunne was 24 – in 1889 – he realised that some of his dreams appeared to give him a glimpse into the future. He dreamed, for example, of a newspaper headline about a volcanic eruption in Martinique in which 4,000 people were killed. He saw the newspaper headline announcing the eruption soon after. However, it mentioned that 40,000 people had been killed, but later proved to be quite wrong about the number. This led Dunne to reason that what he had dreamed about was not the eruption itself, but seeing the newspaper headline with its mistaken figure – he had obviously misread 40,000 as 4,000. After that, he began making a note of his dreams (keeping a pencil and paper beside the bed), and noticed how often he dreamed of the future. His famous book *An Experiment With Time* (1927), was immensely successful and when J. B. Priestley based a series of plays on Dunne's theories, they became even more popular.

Dunne's great contribution was to point out that if we can dream of the future before it has happened, then there is something quite mistaken about our idea of time. Time *must* be some kind of an illusion.

Later, the retired Cambridge don, Tom Lethbridge, repeated Dunne's experiments, keeping a sheet of paper and a pencil by the bed. He noticed how many times he actually dreamed of events that would take place in the future. However, these were not world shaking events but simply things that happened to *him*.

Dream Detective

In 1996, another "dream psychic," Chris Robinson, achieved overnight fame with a publication of a book called *Dream Detective*. In this, his collaborator, journalist Andy Boot, describes how (in 1989), when Chris Robinson was in his late 30s, his life went through a period of violent upheaval. (It seems generally true that "mediums" have difficult childhoods or have been through some kind of traumatic experience which releases their powers.) One night, he woke up hearing the voice of his dead grandmother. The voice told him that someone was trying to steal his car. Unfortunately, since the car was parked five miles away, there was no chance that he could do anything about it. His grandmother remarked, "Don't worry Christopher, I'll do something about it."

The next day, a woman who lived in a caravan where the car was parked told him how, in the middle of the night, her husband had been woken up by a blinding light and a voice. When he looked out of the window, he saw some men trying to break into Chris Robinson's car. He chased them off.

Soon after that, he dreamed that he saw a man swimming in the sea. The man told him that he had fallen off a boat. Two days later, there was a news item about an ex-soldier who had fallen off a ferry and drowned.

A few nights later, Chris dreamed of the ex-soldier again, who told him that he was going to set the ferry alight as a kind of revenge. Chris rang a policeman he knew. And in fact, a fire *did* take place on a ferry – the sister ship of the one the soldier had fallen from. (Most ferries sail "in tandem" with another ferry which starts from the opposite end of the route.)

In his next dream, the ex-soldier told him about an IRA cell in Cheltenham, in which the IRA men were posing as building workers. Again, Chris reported it to the police. Not long afterwards, he proved accurate when the police arrested five IRA men in Cheltenham.

A cache of guns and explosives had been recovered. From there on, Chris Robinson sent a note of his dreams to his police informant.

Typical of the remarkable accuracy of his dreams is a case that occurred in December 1990. He dreamed that a man was being drowned in a bucket of water, gasping for breath as the liquid filled his lungs. By this time, his notes on his dreams had become so much a matter of habit that he did it in a semi-sleeping state. The next morning he found that he had written, "[Urquhy] Baby – drown him in a bucket of water." He became convinced that the killer was a man called Urquhart, and appeared to know by some instinct that the man who was going to be killed was called Patrick Frater. He passed on this information to his police contact. Just over a week later, a man called Danny Frater was shot as he tried to drive away in his car by a man with a shotgun. Fortunately, he was not seriously hurt. The shooting was over a woman. She had previously lived with Danny Frater, and then left him for another man. There had been a violent argument, the result of which led to Danny Frater being shot.

The police soon ascertained that Danny Frater had a criminal record. But his brother, Patrick Frater, seemed to be a law abiding citizen.

Later, Chris again dreamed about the murder of Patrick Frater, and wrote on the paper beside his bed that it would take place in a council estate called Hockwell Ring, somewhere near blocks of flats called Marsh Farm, Lee Bank and Hookers Court.

Two nights later, on January 20, 1990, he dreamed that Patrick Frater was now dead. His police contact checked, but all he could find out was that Patrick's brother, Danny Frater, was still alive and well.

Two nights later, Chris actually dreamed of Patrick Frater – a West Indian, who babbled, "Colin did it, he killed me." This time he was correct. Patrick Frater *was* dead. On that night, January 22, Patrick Frater had been in bed with his girlfriend when there had been a loud hammering on the front door. He had leaned out of the window to see what was happening. A man below had directed a shotgun at him and pulled the trigger. The man who killed him was called Colin Nicholls, and he was the man for whom Danny Frater's girlfriend had left him and with whom he had quarrelled violently. Patrick Frater had been shot by mistake – Nicholls thought that his brother Danny was staying with him, and that it was Danny who had leaned out of the window.

Nicholls had a close friend called Andrew Urquhart, who was known as "Urquhy baby." The pellets had penetrated Patrick Frater's lungs, so that his death was virtually a drowning caused by his own blood.

As result of persistent police work, Colin Nicholls and Andrew Urquhart were both charged – Nicholls with murder, Urquhart with being an accomplice (having driven the car in which Nicholls had escaped.) Nicholls received 15 years, and Urquart four years.

Perhaps the most significant thing about this case is that Chris Robinson dreamed about Patrick Frater again. Frater came back into his dreams to introduce him to another spirit – a black man called Ernie, who wanted to tell Chris that he had *not* (in spite of appearances) committed suicide. Frater had decided to introduce Ernie to Chris Robinson because Robinson had been so successful in his own case. According to Ernie, he had been killed by two men in an empty house, and the death looked like suicide because they had killed him by hanging him.

Robinson's reputation – he had often appeared in the local newspapers in Luton – led a couple named Dulcie and Paul to contact him. Dulcie was the sister of a black man called Ernest Bandoo, who had been found hanging in an empty house. After a quarrel with his wife, Bandoo had stormed out of the house and gone to live in a house that he was decorating nearby. After he had been away for more than two weeks, his sister Dulcie decided to look for him. She and her boyfriend Paul went to the empty house and found Ernie's body, already beginning to decompose.

Oddly enough, Ernie did not want revenge on the two men who had killed him. He felt that it was too late now and that revenge would be pointless. So he refused to name them. He seemed to be contented with the knowledge that his family knew he had not committed suicide.

The strangest thing about these two cases is that Chris Robinson dreamed of the murders weeks before they happened. Yet it was only *after* the deaths of Patrick Frater and Ernie Bandoo that the "spirits" actually talked to him in his dreams.

J. W. Dunne believed that the dream state frees the mind from its normal preoccupation with the present moment and allows it a glimpse of the past and the future. Although Dunne never admitted it during his lifetime, he believed firmly that he was some kind of a "medium" and that this explained his dreams of the future. He had also been convinced from a very early age that he would one day have a very important message to bring to mankind. In fact he was correct – for he was the first to state clearly that time, as human beings know it, is some kind of an illusion.

The strange abilities of Chris Robinson seem to underline the same point. Many "mediums" sink into a trance in order to contact "spirits." Chris Robinson sinks into a dream. But he is totally convinced that in his dreams, he is actually able to contact the spirits of the land. And, if the accounts given by Andy Root in *Dream Detective* are accurate, there seems to be very little doubt that he is correct.

Borley Rectory

The vicarage reputed to be "the most haunted house in England" was built – at Borley, near Sudbury, in Suffolk – in 1863, by the Revd Henry Bull, on the site of a Benedictine abbey. Several people, including Bull's daughters Ethel and Elsie, claimed to have seen a phantom nun gliding along a path known as Nun's Walk; the story was that she had been caught eloping with a monk, and had been bricked up alive.

The Revd Henry Bull's son Harry claimed to have seen a phantom coach. Harry also saw a pair of legs under a fruit tree and, assuming they belonged to a poacher, followed – until they came to a postern gate – then realized the legs had no body attached.

Bull was succeeded in 1927 by the Revd Guy Smith. While Smith and his wife were there, "poltergeist" phenomena began – stone-throwing and phantom foot-steps – and Smith contacted the *Daily Mirror*, who in turn asked the famous "ghostbuster" Harry Price to investi-gate. But the Smiths left after nine months. The next tenant was the Revd Lionel Foyster, married to a much younger wife. And it was while the Foysters were there that Borley's poltergeists kept up a non-stop series of distur-bances – bells ringing, footsteps walking around the house, bricks thrown – Foyster was even awakened by having a jug of water poured over him. The Foysters also claim to have seen ghosts, including the Revd Henry Bull, who built the rectory. One visitor who tried to grab a ghost was hit in the eye.

The Foysters moved out in 1935, and Harry Price – who had been investigating on and off for years – rented the rectory. In 1938, a team experimenting with auto-matic writing were told that it would be burnt down. And that is precisely what happened, in February 1939. In 1943, Harry Price dug in the ruins of the cellar, and found fragments of a human skull, with a badly abscessed jawbone – perhaps this explained why the phantom nun always looked so gloomy.

When Price died in 1948, the Society for Psychical Research published a booklet on his work, throwing doubt on his honesty; this led many people to assume that the Borley haunting had been concocted by Price. Yet no one who has looked closely into the case can believe this. Ghosts were reported more than half a century before Price came on the scene. It is a pity that Price's love of publicity, and his blatant showmanship, led to the subsequent "debunking." The evidence shows that Borley Rectory was, as he claimed, the most haunted house in England.

6

Possession?

The strange case of Doris Fischer – described in Chapter 1 – seems to show that several different "spirits" can live in the same body. But can a spirit actually take over the body of another person? The amazing case of Lurancy Vennum seems to prove that the answer is "yes."

Lurancy Vennum

On July 11, 1877, a 13-year-old girl named Mary Lurancy Vennum (living in Watseka, Illinois), had a fit and was unconscious for five hours. The next day it happened again, but then it became clear that she was in a trance for she declared she could see heaven and the angels as well as a brother and sister who had died. For the next six months, these trances recurred and Lurancy Vennum was apparently "possessed" by a number of disagreable personalities including an old woman called Katrina Hogan. Relatives advised her parents to send her to an insane asylum. But some neighbors named Roth, whose deceased daughter

Mary had also been subject to fits of "insanity," persuaded the Vennums to see a doctor, W.W. Stevens, of Janesville, Wisconsin.

When Stevens first saw Mary Lurancy Vennum on February 1, 1878, the girl was "possessed" by Katrina Hogan, who sat hunched up in a chair staring sulkily into space. When Stevens tried to move closer, she told him sharply to keep his distance. Then she seemed to soften towards him and talked about herself and her parents. (She called her father "Old Black Dick.") Soon the personality changed and the newcomer described himself as a young man named Willie Canning. But he talked disconnectedly and then had a fit. Stevens tried hypnosis and it worked. Lurancy reappeared and explained that she had been possessed by evil spirits. She was still in the state of trance and told them that she was surrounded by spirits, one of whom was called Mary Roth and who wanted to come.

Mr Roth, who was in the room, said, "That is my daughter. Mary Roth is my girl. Why, she has been in heaven 12 years. Yes, let her come, we'll be glad to have her come." Lurancy apparently took counsel with the spirits and then announced that Mary would come and take over her body. Soon after that, Lurancy woke up.

The next morning, Lurancy's father called at the office of Asa Roth and told him that Lurancy was now claiming to be Mary Roth and that Mary was asking to go home. "She seems like a child – real homesick, wanting to see her pa and ma and her brothers."

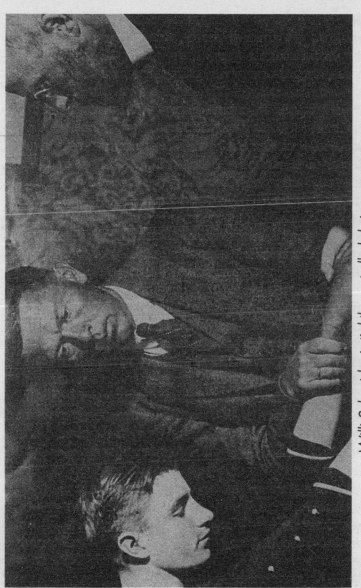

Willi Schneider is tightly controlled during a seance.

Mary's case history resembled in many ways that of Lurancy Vennum – and even more like that of the Seeress of Prevorst, Friederike Hauffe. Mary had also started to suffer from fits at the age of six months and one day in a state of depression, she had cut her arm with a knife until she fainted. Five days of raving mania followed after which she recognized no one and seemed to lose all her senses, but when blindfolded could read and do everything, as if she could see. After a few days, she returned to her normal condition but the fits became worse and she died in one of them in July 1865, 12 years before Lurancy's "possession." Her clairvoyant powers had been attested by many prominent people in Watseka.

Before Lurancy – or rather "Mary" – could be taken to the Roth's home, Mrs Roth and her daughter, Minerva, came to call at the Vennums. "Mary" was looking out of the window as they came along the street and said, "Why there comes Ma and my sister Nervie!" When they came in she flung her arms round their necks and burst into tears of joy.

The Vennums were understandably reluctant to let their daughter go but "Mary" became so homesick that they finally agreed. On February 11, 1878, she was taken back to the Roths' home. On the way there, they passed the house in which the Roths had lived at the time Mary was alive. "Mary" insisted that this was her home and had to be persuaded that her family no longer lived there. When they arrived at the new home Mary said, "Why there's our old piano and the same old piano cover." She greeted the crowd of relatives who were waiting there with plain signs of recognition. A Mrs Wagner, who (under the name of Mary Lord), had been Mary Roth's Sunday school teacher was greeted with the words, "Oh, Mary Lord, you've changed the least of anyone." She told them that "the angels" would allow her to stay until some time in May – three months ahead.

Her family were naturally anxious to test her and asked her all kinds of questions. "Mary" soon convinced them – she was able to describe hundreds of incidents in the life of the former Mary Roth. She described in detail her stay at a water-cure place in Peoria. Asked if she remembered an incident when the stove pipe fell and burnt Frank, she was able to point out the exact place on the arm where Frank was burnt. Asked about an old dog, she showed them the spot where it had died. When she talked about slashing, her arm with a knife, she started to roll up her sleeve to show Dr Stevens the scar, then recollected that she was not in the same body. "It's not this arm – it's the one in the ground." After her death, her parents had tried to communicate with her by means of a "medium." Mary was able to tell them the message she wrote out for them through the "medium," Sam, giving the exact time and place.

One of the most convincing incidents occurred when Mrs Roth found an old velvet head-dress that Mary had worn during her lifetime. Mary's father suggested leaving it out on the hall stand. "Mary" came in from the yard and immediately said, "Why, there's my old head-dress that I wore when my hair was short." This reminded her of a box of letters and when her mother brought this, she found one of her collars. "Look, here's that old collar I tatted."

Myers, who describes the case in the second chapter of *Human Personality*, says, "During her stay at Mr Roth's her physical condition continually improved, being under the care and treatment of her supposed parents and the advice and help of her physician. She was ever obedient to the government and rules of the family, like a careful and wise child, always keeping in the company of some of the family, unless visiting the nearest neighbors across the street. She was often invited and went with Mrs Roth to visit the first families of the city, who soon became satisfied that the girl was not crazy, but a fine, well-mannered child."

Mary told her family that she could stay with them until May 21, 1878. On that morning her mother wrote, "Mary is to leave the body of Rancy today, about eleven o'clock." "Mary went around saying goodbye to neighbors, hugged and kissed her parents and then set out for Lurancy Vennum's house. On the way, "Mary" vanished and Lurancy returned. She recognized all the members of her own family and was apparently delighted to be back in her own surroundings.

Four years later, Lurancy married a farmer called George Binning. Her parents discouraged her from using her mediumship in case it brought back the "fits," but Mary Roth often "dropped in" when her own parents were there and seemed quite unchanged from her previous visit. When Lurancy had her first baby, Mary even put her into a trance so that she would not suffer the pains of childbirth.

Richard Hodgson, the skeptical young member of the Society for Psychical Research, who had become famous when he "exposed" Mme Blavatsky in 1885, heard about the case when he was in America and instantly saw that, if genuine, it was a practically watertight proof of life after death. He interviewed all the principal characters except Lurancy herself, who had moved west with her husband. In spite of this disappointment, Hodgson ended totally convinced of the truth of the incident as narrated by Dr Stevens and the various family members and friends. He agreed that this could be a case of multiple personality but felt, on the whole, that all the evidence pointed to a genuine case of "possession" of Lurancy by the deceased Mary Roth.

The Alexandrina Case

Another of the early classic cases – unfortunately never investigated by a trained researcher like Hodgson – has become known as the Alexandrina case.

On March 15, 1910, a five-year-old girl named Alexandrina Samona died in Palermo, Sicily. Her mother, Adela, wife of Dr Carmelo Samona – was distraught with grief. But three days after the death, she had a dream in which Alexandrina told her not to mourn because she was going to return. She showed her mother an embryo. Adela Samona dismissed the dream, knowing that an ovarian operation had made it almost impossible for her to have children.

A few days later, when Adela was sadly recalling the

child to her husband, three loud knocks were heard. The parents began to attend seances and two "spirits" spoke through the "medium" – one claiming to be the child Alexandrina, the other an aunt who had died long ago. "Alexandrina, told her mother that she would be reborn before Christmas as one of twins. In fact, twin girls were born to Adela Samona on November 22, 1910, just over nine months after Alexandrina's deaths. The two girls were of totally different personalities, but one of them had two small birthmarks in the same place as the dead child – she was also, like Alexandrina, left-handed. The parents named her after the dead child. In personality, this second Alexandrina was very like the first, introverted, tidy, disposed to spend most of her time folding clothes and linen.

What finally convinced the parents that the child was a reincarnation of the dead Alexandrina was an incident that happened when the twins were ten. They were told that they were going on an outing to the town of Monreale – neither of them had been there. But Alexandrina insisted that she had been there with her mother in the company of a "lady with horns." She also described the statue on the roof of the church and described some "red priests" that they had seen there. In fact, Adela Samona *had* taken her first daughter Alexandrina to Monreale not long before her death, in the company of a woman who had some unsightly cysts on her forehead. They had been to the church and had seen some priests from Greece who wore red robes. Dr Samona was so struck by this evidence of reincarnation that he went to some trouble to put the case on record, together with the depositions of various witnesses, and published it in the periodical, *Filosofia de la Scienza.*

In the mid-1960s, Dr Ian Stevenson of the University of Virginia, began publishing the results of some of his own painstaking investigations into cases of apparent reincarnation. His *Twenty Cases Suggestive of Reincarnation* (1966), has become a classic as have the subsequent three volumes *Cases of the Reincarnation Type* (1975–1980.) One of the cases recalls that of Lurancy Vennum.

Jasbir Lal Jat

In 1954, a three-year-old boy named Jasbir Lal Jat died of smallpox. Before he could be buried the next day, the corpse stirred and revived. It was some weeks before the child could speak and when he did, his parents were astonished that his personality had changed completely. Jasbir had been a rather dull, quiet little boy. He had suddenly become more lively. He announced that he was the son of a Brahmin family (a higher caste than his present family), who lived in the village of Vehedi and he refused to eat food unless it was cooked by a Brahmin. He said that he had been poisoned by doctored sweets and had fallen off a cart and smashed his skull, as a result of which he died. Jasbir's family were understandably skeptical, assuming that his illness had affected his mind. But they began to reconsider in 1957, when a Brahmin lady from Vehedi came to Jasbir's village and

145

he instantly recognized her as his aunt. Jasbir was taken back to Vehedi, and, like Mary Roth, showed detailed knowledge of his former residence, escorting a party on a tour. His name in the previous existence had been Sobha Ram, and his detailed knowledge of his life convinced everyone that Jasbir and Sobha Ram were the same person. The accusation about the poisoned sweets was never satisfactorily cleared up – Sobha Ram was said to have died of smallpox.

The most fascinating point about this case, of course, is that Jasbir was already three when he "died" and was "taken over" by Sobha Ram, *who died at the same time*. The implication is that Sobha Ram was able to slip into the body before brain death had occurred and fight his way back to life.

Sumitra Singh

Another of Stevenson's cases also involves a murder and is as astonishing (in its own way), as that of Lurancy Vennum.

The girl concerned was a young Hindu woman named Sumitra Singh, born in 1968. At the age of thirteen, she married a man called Jagdish and went to live with him in his family home in a village called Sharifpura, in Uttar Pradesh.

Sumitra's family was poor and she herself never went to school. Early in 1985, not long after having a baby, Sumitra began to suffer from spells of dizziness or trance. Her eyes would roll upwards and her teeth would clench. And, just like Lurancy Vennum, she

During the Victorian age, number 50 Berkeley Square (in London's West End), was one of the most famous haunted houses – largely due to Bulwer Lytton's famous story, "The Haunted and the Haunters." Lytton's hero agrees to spend a night in the haunted house and is subjected to all kinds of terrifying manifestations.

It is not clear how number 50 (now numbered 25), Berkeley Square gained its gruesome reputation. From the 1840s onwards, there were reports of strange noises coming from the house and neighbors said they could hear the sound of heavy boxes or furniture being dragged across bare floorboards. It soon had a reputation for being haunted by a ghost "too horrible to describe," others said that it was "shapeless and slimy and emitted gruesome slopping noises" as it went up and down the stairs.

For several decades now, the house has been occupied by a firm of antique booksellers, "Maggs Brothers," who insist that they have never had the slightest reason to believe the place to be haunted.

seemed to be taken over by different personalities while she was in this state. One of them claimed to be a woman who had drowned herself in a well and another a man from another Indian state.

In July 1985, while she was in a trance, Sumitra predicted that she would die in three days time. And in fact, she fell into a trance then and seemed to die showing no sign of pulse or breathing. Because the village was very poor, there was no doctor who could come along and check whether she was dead.

Some time later, Sumitra began to breathe and open her eyes. She seemed confused and spoke very little. But when finally she started to talk, her family thought she had gone mad. Because she now declared that her name was not Sumitra, but Shiva, and that she had been murdered by her in-laws in the small town of Dibiyapur. She did not recognize the people around her bed and refused to accept her husband and child. In the course of the next few days, she added many details about her life as "Shiva."

Now in fact, there had been a young married woman named Shiva Diwedi, who had lived in the small town of Dibiyapur. She had been about six years older than Sumitra and her father was a college professor. Shiva had a good education and graduated with a degree. At the age of 18, she had married a man named Chedi Lal and moved with her husband into the house of her in-laws in Dibiyapur. There she had two children, named Tinku and Rinku. But her in-laws objected when Shiva said she wanted to return to sit her final examinations and when her uncle visited her, Shiva told him that her mother-in-law and one of her sisters-in-law had beaten her.

That night, Shiva was found dead lying by the railway line. Her husband's family said that she must have committed suicide. In fact, her only injury was a bruise on the head. It seemed unlikely that this had been caused by a passing train – it would have caused far more severe injuries. The uncle who had visited her asked her husband's family to delay cremation until he could fetch her father. But they ignored him and Shiva was cremated with indecent haste the next day.

Understandably, Shiva's father – whose name was Ram Siya Tripathi believed that his daughter had been murdered.

And this was exactly the story that the young lady who called herself "Shiva" told her new family. She said that her sister-in-law had hit her on the head with a brick and that they then carried her body to the railway line to make it look like suicide. Oddly enough, this had happened two months before Sumitra's death.

The two villages were 100 miles apart and it was by pure chance that Shiva's father, living in Dibiyapur, heard that a girl living 100 miles away was claiming to be his daughter who had been murdered.

Eventually, Shiva's father made the journey to Sharifpura and met the woman who claimed to be his daughter. Shiva recognized him immediately and he himself was convinced that she was his daughter.

He took her back to Dibiyapur. There she immediately recognized members of her family and when she looked through an album of family photographs, was able to identify everybody in them correctly. And when she looked at a picture of herself at the age of five, she simply said; "This is me." When shown pictures of her two children, Tinku and Rinku, she said they were her own children and began to cry. When she was shown a photograph of her sister-in-law Rama Kanti she said immediately; "This is Rama Kanti, who hit me with the brick."

Her father, now completely convinced that Shiva was his daughter and that she had been murdered, filed a charge of murder against her husband's family.

The husband and father-in-law were arrested, but the police had to release them because of a lack of evidence. The sister, Rama Kanti, denied killing Shiva with a brick but nevertheless went into hiding for several months.

Back in Sumitra's home village, it seemed that the period among her own family had completely wiped out Shiva's memory of Sumitra's family. She did not seem to recognize any of them. She did not even recognize a cousin with whom she had stayed for eight years and who had taught her the rudiments of reading and writing.

The villagers of Sharifpura noticed that "Sumitra" seemed to have changed completely. The uneducated girl now behaved like an educated woman of a higher caste. She could read and write Hindi and behaved like a woman of culture. Yet gradually, her rejection of her husband and baby melted away. Although she often referred to Tinku and Rinku, she now commented; "If I look after this child, God will take care of them. If I neglect this child, would God not punish me?"

Oddly enough, during the autumn of 1986, Shiva suddenly became confused and during a period of a few hours, Sumitra reemerged. But at the end of this brief period, Shiva reappeared and once again took control of the body.

The case was carefully investigated by Ian Stevenson and two of his colleagues, who interviewed various family members and came to the conclusion that there was certainly no reason to think that the case was a hoax or that Sumitra herself was suffering herself from some kind of amnesia in which she thought she was somebody else – the character of Shiva was far too complex for the imagination of a simple village girl. On the whole, the investigators were inclined to accept that Shiva *was* another personality who had somehow taken over Sumitra's body.

That obviously poses some interesting questions. The fact that Sumitra "came back" briefly in the autumn of 1986 makes it look as if perhaps Sumitra was still living in the same body but "repressed," like some of the personalities we considered in Chapter 1. There is also the puzzling fact that Shiva died two months before Sumitra – it looks as if her "spirit" was wandering around before it found a body it was able to take over. In that case, is it possible that Sumitra agreed to be "possessed" by Shiva, in the same way that Lurancy allowed herself to be "possessed" by Mary Roth?

Uttara Huddar

One of the strangest cases ever investigated by Stevenson was that of a young girl called Uttara Huddar, who was a teacher at Nagpur University. Uttara was "taken over" by a young woman who had apparently died more than 100 years before of snake-bite and who found the modern world completely bewildering.

Uttara was born in 1941 and her mother later told one of the investigators that during her pregnancy she had had a recurrent dream of being bitten on her right toe by a snake. But this dream went away after she gave birth to Uttara. She insists that she never told Uttara about it.

India has many languages and the one Uttara spoke is called Marathi. In due course, she obtained a bachelor's degree in biology, then taught at various high schools. She went on to take a masters degree in English and Public Administration. Then she was appointed part-time lecturer at Nagpur University. So far, Uttara's life had been perfectly normal. But when she was 24, the first sign of problems began to appear on the horizon. She met an ex-schoolfellow and decided she wanted to marry him. But apparently he was not interested. She began practising meditation at this time and a few years later, still tormented by strong emotions, she tried to find an outlet for her frustrations in even deeper meditation. She wrote, "A hurricane-like force swept me off and liberated me completely from the attraction towards F." (Her ex-schoolfellow.) She also met a homeopathic doctor, a man in his 50s, with whom she fell in love. He was treating her for poor health and once again, her thoughts turned towards marriage. Once again, she was to be disappointed.

It was at this period that she went into an ashram and began meditating more deeply than ever before. And it was during this period that another personality began to appear – a young girl called Sharada, who had died at the age of 24, when she was bitten in the right toe by a snake.

The strange thing is that Sharada spoke another Indian language, Bengali, of which Uttara did not speak a word. So when Sharada took over her body, Uttara began to speak in a totally different language. On one occasion, Sharada stayed for as long as 43 days. But she always disappeared again and Uttara once again was able to take over her body.

Sometimes, Uttara would have a sensation that ants were crawling over her head and Sharada would take over a few hours later. But sometimes, Uttara fell asleep at night and simply woke up as Sharada. The most interesting part of this story is Sharada's reaction to the modern world.

From various clues, Stevenson eventually came to the conclusion that Sharada had died in 1829 at the age of 24. When she began to take over Uttara's body in 1974, she was baffled by kitchen utensils, gas stoves, cars and trains. At first, of course, she could not understand a word spoken by her new family, since they spoke Marathi and she spoke Bengali – in an old dialect form that contained no words that had entered the language after about 1830. Eventually, she picked up a little Marathi and Uttari's parents picked up a little Bengali and they were able to converse. She said that in her day, people were transported about by horses, boats, bullock carts and litters carried by men. When shown a glass jar, she was amazed at the strange substance since, in her day, all the jars in the kitchen were made of earthenware. The foods she asked for were those that had been eaten in Bengal and not in the place where she now found herself living – Mahaashtra.

When speaking with Bengali speakers, Sharada was often totally bewildered by the words they used –

words which had not existed in her day. The same was true when she read books written in Bengali. She used phrases which are not used today – although they were in the early nineteenth century – and she wrote many letters as they used to be written in old Bengali manuscript. She also wrote the Bengali alphabet counter-clockwise which children in the early nineteenth century were taught to do but which is no longer used. Once she was shocked by a Bengali expression which had completely changed its meaning since the early nineteenth century, and which in her day had a vulgar meaning. (When Coleridge wrote in "Kubla Khan", "As if this earth in thick, fast pants were breathing", he would certainly not have understood why the line brings a smile to the face of modern schoolchildren.)

Sharada claimed to be a doctor's wife and that her mother was the daughter of a learned man who lived in Burdwan in Bengal. She was 24 and pregnant, when she had been taken by her husband to the house of an aunt in Saptagram and it was there, while picking flowers in the garden, that she was bitten on her toe by a poisonous snake and died.

She often spoke unfavorably about the East India Company, which ruled Bengal in those days and said how much she hated the Company and its soldiers. When one of the researchers asked what was her husband's name she said, "Was? *Is.*" And when he explained that her husband was no longer alive, she began to cry. Typically, she refused to pronounce her husband's name – which was not customary when she was alive – but would only write it down.

154

At first, she did not know anything about taps and when shown the water system and tap said, "In our place we use a pond." She bathed and washed her hair in cold water, drying herself with one end of her wet sari, after wringing out the water. Then visitors came, she covered her head with her sari, and sometimes asked them if the roads were good, or if they had come by bullock cart. Once when a female investigator saw her looking with interest at her gold-plated bangle, she asked Sharada if she would like to have it, and Sharada replied: "How can I? It has to come from my mother-in-law." Enquiry revealed that, in fact, this was the Bengali custom when she had been alive.

Sharada's genuineness was strikingly proved when she gave a list of her father's family, naming her great-great-grandfather, great-grandfather, grandfather, father, two uncles and two step-brothers. Their name, she said, was Chatto Padhyawa. The investigators were able to trace the family – and learned that the present head of the family had a genealogy of the family which dated back to the early nineteenth century. It showed that Sharada was amazingly accurate. It also showed that, as she claimed, she came from a family of learned men (pundits.)

Sharada continued to appear, and to temporarily take over Uttara's body, until 1983. After that, her appearances became less and less frequent. It seems clear, that somewhere deep in Uttara's mind, Sharada continues to live.

The case is puzzling. The fact that Uttara's mother dreamed about being bitten in the right toe by a snake during her pregnancy, and the fact that Uttara herself was always terrified of snakes as a child, might suggest that Uttara had Sharada living inside her from the moment she was born – or conceived. Which leads to the interesting question: how many more of us are walking around with long-dead people living inside us, waiting for the opportunity to express themselves?

7

What is a Ghost?

What, then, is a ghost? All the evidence appears to show that it is a person who is dead and does not realize it.

Carl Wickland was a Los Angeles doctor who had been born in Sweden in 1861. He married and quickly discovered that his wife was an excellent "medium" (or "psychic intermediary" as he called it), and frequently went into a trance, during which voices that claimed to spirits spoke through her. They had married young and one day, while Wickland was still a student, he took part in the dissection of a body at the medical school. When he returned home, his wife seemed to feel faint and staggered as if she was going to fall. But when he placed his hand on her shoulder, she suddenly drew herself up and said threateningly, "What do you mean by cutting me?" When Wickland protested that he was not cutting anyone, the voice said, "Of course you are! You are cutting on my leg!" Wickland then realized that this was the owner of the body, and that the spirit had followed him home.

When Wickland made his wife sit in a chair, the

spirit objected that he had no right to touch him. When Wickland said that he had a perfect right to touch his own wife, the spirit replied, "Your wife! What are you talking about! I'm no woman – I'm a man."

Wickland pointed out that if the man was sitting there in an armchair, then they could not be cutting up his body in the college. At this, the spirit said, "I guess I must be what they call dead, so I won't have any more use for my old body. If you can learn anything by cutting it up, go ahead." After that, it begged for a chew of tobacco or a pipe, but since Mrs Wickland detested them both, Wickland was forced to refuse. Finally, says Wickland, the spirit realized that it was dead and left.

Wickland says that the next day, he examined the teeth of the corpse and could see that the man had been a heavy user of tobacco. This showed Wickland that a "ghost" may believe that it is still alive – particularly if death came unexpectedly. He also encountered a case that seemed to demonstrate that spirits did not need to manifest themselves through a "medium." When he was alone one day, dissecting a female corpse, he thought he heard a distant voice shouting, "Don't murder me!" A newspaper on the floor made a rustling noise, as if it was being crushed. Some days later, at a seance, a spirit who gave her name as Minnie Morgan claimed that it was she who shouted, "Don't murder me" and crushed the newspaper. Minnie also had to be convinced that she was no longer alive.

At seances, entities who spoke through his wife

Mr Daniels is controlled by one of his regular guides during a trance circle at a Muswell Hill house.

explained to Wickland that such "homeless spirits" – those who are unaware that they are dead – are attracted by the warmth of the "human aura" (a kind of energy sphere which is supposed to surround the human body), and, under certain circumstances, may attach themselves to its owner as a kind of mental parasite. In effect, such spirits are in a state of sleep, in which dreams and reality are confused and – as in sleep – the dreamer is unaware that he is dreaming.

These spirits are usually known as "earth bound spirits." And since the nineteenth century, groups of people who call themselves "rescue circles" have attempted to speak to such spirits and free them from their "earth bound" state.

One of the most remarkable modern examples is the case of the Enfield poltergeist, described by psychical researcher, Guy Playfair, in his book *This House is Haunted*. Mrs Harper, who rented the house, lived there with her four children, whose ages ranged from 13 to seven. She was separated from her husband.

The manifestations started in August 1977, when the beds of two of the children began to shake. The next evening, a chair moved of its own accord. When journalists came to the house to investigate, the poltergeist threw a Lego brick at the photographer and bruised him above the eye.

Playfair and his friend Maurice Grosse went to the house at the request of the Society for Psychical Research, and spent two years investigating, seeing all kinds of extraordinary phenomena, including one of the girls (still fast asleep), being "levitated" in the middle of the room in her nightdress. When Playfair tried communicating with the "spirit" by rapping, it rapped back. But when Playfair asked, "Don't you realize you are dead?" there was a violent crash and they rushed upstairs to find a bedroom in chaos with objects scattered all over it. When one of the children tried to go upstairs, the ghost literally pulled her leg – she was found standing there on the stairs, her legs stretched out behind her, firmly held by an invisible hand.

Eventually, the poltergeist began to speak – an extremely rare occurrence in such cases – and identified itself as Joe Watson, a man who had died in the house. Asked, "Where do you come from?" he replied, "From the graveyard." In fact, there was a graveyard very close by. Soon, another "spirit" began to speak, identifying itself as Bill who had died in the house of a haemorrhage as he was asleep in a chair.

Eventually, the "haunting" was stopped by a Dutch psychic named Dono Gmelig-Meyling. He apparently somehow contacted the entities, who seemed to have agreed to go away. At one point in the investigation, Playfair remarks that, "It looks as if we had half the local graveyard at one time or another."

Playfair's own explanation was that the absence of the father made it a thoroughly unhappy household, full of some kind of negative psychic energy and that "spirits" from the local graveyard were able to wander in and out of the house and take advantage of this energy to manifest themselves.

Knebworth House was the home of Lord Lytton, the famous Victorian novelist. A room known as "the red and gold chamber" had such a bad reputation among the servants that they always avoided it.

In 1880, seven years after Lytton's death, an American actress called Mary Anderson had personal experience of the ghost of "the red and gold room." She was a friend of the then Lady Lytton, and during a tour of Great Britain she was invited to Knebworth to relax for a few days. Her account of what happened was subsequently related to the American drama critic, William Winter, who published it in a book called *Other Days* (1908.)

That evening in 1880, there had been a party at Knebworth and Miss Anderson had joined in a parlour game that called for the players to jot down the names of all the famous people they could remember beginning with a certain letter of the alphabet. Mary Anderson had got stuck at "A" – the only name she could think of was her own. She went to bed immediately after the game was ended. Her bedroom, "the red and gold chamber," was hung with red and gold tapestries. The bed was a magnificent four-poster with heavy curtains and a canopy.

Mary Anderson got into bed but was unable to get to sleep. She kept trying to remember names beginning with A. At 2.00 a.m., tired but unable to fall asleep, she was suddenly jerked wide awake by a sound like clothing brushing against the tapestried wall. Then she heard the sound of feet. She tried to scream but could only manage a kind of whisper. A moment later, she says, she heard a "deep and pathetic sigh." It seemed to come from the foot of the bed and a moment later, she felt herself being grasped by the shoulders and held down against the pillow. With tremendous effort, she managed to call for the maid who had been assigned the small adjoining room. At that moment, the invisible hands suddenly ceased to grip her shoulders. When the maid came into the room, she was obviously terrified. "Have you seen it, Miss?" She too had been held fast to the bed by a pair of hands. The two women lost no time in getting dressed and hurrying down to stay in the room of the Lytton governess for the night.

The next morning, when Mary Anderson told the story at breakfast, she was surprised that her host and hostess reacted without the astonishment she expected. Later, she learned from a servant that the room was supposed to be haunted by the spirit of the first Lord Lytton. Mary Anderson remained convinced that she had been held down by the ghost of the famous Victorian writer himself.

We began Chapter 1 by raising the question of whether it is possible for the human personality to exist outside the physical body. This book should have provided ample evidence that it is. In fact, an enormous number of people have experienced what is known as an "out-of-the-body experience", in which they experience the sensation of floating clear of the body. There are literally thousands of records of "OBEs."

In 1958, an American businessman called Robert Monroe was lying on his living-room couch, when he suddenly felt as if he had been "struck by a beam of warm light," which caused his body to vibrate. He went to see a doctor but the doctor could find nothing wrong with him. One day, lying in bed with his hand hanging over the side of the bed, he had the curious sensation of being able to push his fingertips through the rug and then through the floor beneath. Four weeks later, there was "a surge that seemed to be in my head." When he opened his eyes, he found that he was floating close to the ceiling. Down below, on the bed, was his body. With the shock of desperation, he plunged down towards his body and, to his relief, found that he could merge into it. The experiences continued – an X-ray revealed that he did not have a brain tumor, as he had suspected – and a psychiatrist friend assured him that he was not psychotic.

Little by little, he became accustomed to the experience of leaving his body – it only ever happened when he was lying down – and confirmed, to his own satisfaction, that it was not some kind of imaginary experience. For example, he called on a friend who was supposed to be ill in bed and found him leaving his house with his wife. Later, the friend confirmed that he had decided that he felt well enough to get up and take a walk. Monroe actually pinched one woman friend, who reacted sharply. Later she showed him the bruise on the spot where he had pinched her.

Monroe describes his experiences in three remarkable books, *Journeys Out of the Body*, *Far Journeys*, and *The Ultimate Journey*. These have all become classics of their kind. In 1960, Monroe decided to form an institute for the study of "out-of-the-body" experiences. And there, at the Monroe Institute in Virginia, he was soon able to verify that hundreds of people seem to have this peculiar ability to leave their bodies behind. Eventually, Monroe discovered that all kinds of interesting mental experience could be induced by a technique involving sounds played into both ears.

This depends upon the discovery made in the nineteenth century (but fully explored in the second half of the twentieth century), that human beings have, in effect, two brains inside their heads. The left hemisphere of the human brain is our "practical side" – it deals with language, with everyday problems, with calculation, and with "coping" in general. The right brain, on the other hand, is concerned with shapes and patterns and with such things as the perception of beauty and of meaning. One of the strangest discoveries is that the person you call "you" seems to live in the left brain. A few centimetres away, there seems to be another person of whom you are usually unaware.

Sometimes, an operation is performed to split the brain down the middle – for example, to cure people of epilepsy. The brain, seen from above, looks rather like a walnut, with a kind of bridge dividing its two halves. This bridge is made of nerves and is called the *corpus callosum*. And when the *corpus callosum* is severed, it has the strange effect of turning the patient into two persons.

For example, one "split-brain patient" was shown an indecent picture with her left eye – which is connected to the right brain – while the other eye was unable to see the picture. The girl blushed. Asked why she was blushing, she replied, "I don't know." It was her *other* self (in the right brain), which was responding with embarrassment, while her everyday self (living in the left brain), was unaware what was causing her to blush.

In other words, the two halves of our brain are somehow "out of sync," and Monroe discovered a simple method to synchronise them. Two different sounds of slightly different wave-length are played through two earphones placed over the patient's ears. After a while, this has the strange effect of causing the brain to resolve the conflict by somehow synchronising its two halves.

Visitors to the Monroe Institute quickly discovered that the result was a state of deep relaxation, in which they were able to achieve mental states that are normally rare. For example, many people had a strong impression that they were able to see their past lives. Others were able to "project" themselves to other places and see what was happening there. And many found that they were soon able to have controlled "out-of-the-body" experiences.

Has Monroe really discovered a simple method of achieving OBEs or is it merely imagination? Psychologists – and parapsychologists – have still not made up their minds. But thousands of people who have been to the Monroe Institute have no doubt whatever that Monroe has proved, once and for all, that the human mind – or soul – is independent of the physical body and that it is possible to learn to achieve an "out-of-the-body" experience at will.

If so, man may be standing on the threshold of one of the most interesting and important discoveries in human history.

Index

Alexandrina case 143–5
animal magnetism 55, 79
apparitions 1–3, 97–9
automatic writing 14, 80, 85, 95, 122

Balfour, Arthur 87, 88, 90–6
Basa, Teresita 114–20
"Bell witch" 34–5
Bender, Hans 41–2
Berkeley Square 147
Bettiscombe House 96–7
Borley Rectory 96, 135–6
Branston, Brian 40
Brougham, Lord Henry 2–3, 16–17, 104

Cahagnet, Alphonse 83–4
Chenoweth, Mrs 14–15
Cock Lane ghost 32–4
Cohen, David 21, 23, 27
Cox, Esther 37–8
Cracknell, Robert 123, 124–6
Crowe, Catherine 39, 63–4, 67

Davenport brothers 75
Davis, Andrew Jackson 74
death, persons seen at the moment of 1, 2–3, 98–9
Dee, Dr John 74
doppelgängers 43, 99–102
dowsing 46–7
dream psychics 109, 110, 129–35
Drury, Dr Edward 65–7
Dunne, J.W. 129–30, 134–5

Dyer, Ernest 109–10

Enfield poltergeist 160–1
Epworth poltergeist ("Old Jeffrey") 31–2, 65, 74
Erskine, Lord 4, 16
exorcism 30, 48

Fischer, Doris 5–16
Fodor, Nandor 35, 39
Forthuny, Pascal 121–2
Fox sisters 68–72, 74, 75

ghost detectives 105–35
ghost hunters 87–104
Goethe 100–2

Hauffe, Frederike 57–9
hauntings 65–71
Hayden, Mrs W.R. 78
Hodgson, Richard 15, 143
Hubbell, Walter 37, 38
Huddar, Uttara 151–6
human aura 160
Hydesville manifestation 68–72, 75
hypnosis 24, 55, 83–4

Jung-Stilling, Heinrich 55, 56

Kelly, Edward 74
Kerner, Justinus 56–7, 58, 59
Knebworth House 162–3
Koons, Jonathan 76

Lal Jat, Jasbir 145–6

Landru, Henri 121
Lang, Andrew 38, 90–1
Lashley, David 128–9
Lethbridge, Tom 51, 130
levitation 75, 77, 160–1
life after death 51, 53, 104, 143
Lombroso, Cesare 38–9

McDonnell, Patricia 17–19
Marryat, Captain Frederick 20–1
Meadows-Taylor, Colonel Philip
    1–2, 3, 16, 104
mediums 14–15, 74–5, 76, 82, 92,
    94, 111, 113–14, 122, 131, 135,
    144, 157
Mesmer, Franz Anton 55, 79
mesmerism 55
Monroe, Robert 163–5, 166
multiple personality syndrome
    5–16, 17–19, 21–7
Myers, Frederic 87, 91–2

out-of-body experiences 163–6

personality fragments 35, 38–9
phantom drummer of Tedworth
    30–1
Playfair, Guy 45–6, 47, 51, 96–7,
    160–1
Podmore, Frank 38, 71
poltergeist voices 34, 35, 161
poltergeists 29–52, 59, 60, 72–3, 74,
    81, 82–3, 135, 160–1
Pontefract poltergeist (the black
    monk) 42–4, 47–51
possession 59–60, 117–18, 137–56
precognition 51
Prince, Walter Franklin 4–5, 8, 9, 10,
    11, 12, 13, 14, 15
psychic detectives 120–30
psychic powers 53–8, 63, 101–2
psychometry 51, 120–3
Puckering, John 76

Raynham Hall 20–1
Red Barn murder 107–8
reincarnation 82, 83–4, 144–5

rescue circles 160
Rivail, Denizard-Hyppolyte-Leon
    (Allan Kardec) 79–83, 84, 86
Roberts, Estelle 111–13
Robinson, Chris 130–4, 135
Rosenheim poltergeist 41–2
Ruskin, John 88

seances 75, 78, 158, 160
Seeress of Prevorst 56–9, 63, 81
shamans 53
Shelley, Percy Bysshe 43–4
Shepherd, Janie 123–6, 128–9
Showery, Allan 116, 118–20
Sidgwick, Professor Henry 87, 92
Singh, Sumitra 146–51
Society for Psychical Research 30,
    38, 51, 87–8, 97, 160
spirit guides 62–4, 122–3
"spirit photographs" 21
"spirit teachings" 59, 86
spirits 15, 46, 50–1, 59–60, 73–4, 75–
    6, 78, 81–3, 86, 102, 123, 135,
    144, 160–1
The Spirits' Book 80–1, 83
Spiritualism 68, 73, 74, 84, 86
Stevenson, Dr Ian 145, 150, 153
stone-throwing 29–30, 37
Sutro, Alfred 105–6
Swedenborg, Emanuel 53–5

"table-turning" 78–9
"tape-recording" theory 51
telepathy 51
Tinsley, Mona 110–14
Tombe, Eric 109–10
Tower of London 126

unconscious mind 39, 40, 41, 80

Vennum, Lurancy 137–43
Verner, Dr Heinrich 62, 63, 102
Victoria, Queen 78–9

Weisl, Frieda 39
Wickland, Carl 157–8, 160
Willington Mill 65–7, 68